Scott Foresman

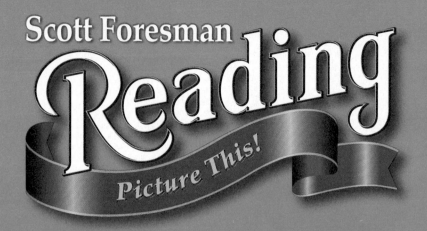

Scott Foresman Reading

Picture This!

Picture This!

From Past to Present

Are We There Yet?

Imagination.kids

Scott Foresman

About the Cover Artist

Jui Ishida works to free her mind when she paints and to paint faster than she can think. Because of this, Ishida feels her painting are full of happy accidents. When people ask her how she did it, she always tells them, "That's my secret."

ISBN 0-328-03936-5

2 3 4 5 6 7 8 9 10 V063 10 09 08 07 06 05 04 03 02

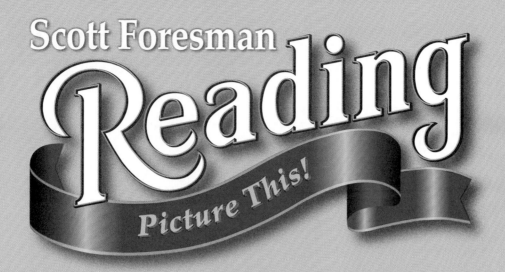

Scott Foresman Reading

Picture This!

Program Authors

Peter Afflerbach

James Beers

Camille Blachowicz

Candy Dawson Boyd

Wendy Cheyney

Deborah Diffily

Dolores Gaunty-Porter

Connie Juel

Donald Leu

Jeanne Paratore

Sam Sebesta

Karen Kring Wixson

Editorial Offices: Glenview, Illinois • Parsippany, New Jersey • New York, New York
Sales Offices: Parsippany, New Jersey • Duluth, Georgia • Glenview, Illinois
Coppell, Texas • Ontario, California

Unit 4 • Contents

From Past to Present

Unit 5 • Contents

Are We There Yet?

6

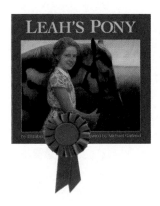

Unit 6 • Contents

Imagination.
kids

From Past to Present

How can our traditions and the traditions of others make our lives more interesting?

Theme

- A **theme** of a story is a big idea of the story.

- When you read a story, think about what the writer wants you to learn or understand from the story.

- You can use something from your own life to help you understand this theme or big idea.

Read "The Coyote and the Goat" from *Doctor Coyote* by John Bierhorst.

Talk About It

1. The theme of this story is stated in the last sentence. What do you think it means?

2. Another theme of this story might be *Look before you leap.* What from your own life helps you understand what this means?

The Coyote and the Goat

a Native American Aesop's Fable retold by John Bierhorst

Traveling along, Coyote met White Beard, and the two of them traveled together.

When Coyote and White Beard got thirsty, they jumped into a well. They drank their fill; then White Beard began looking around to see how he could get back out.

"Don't worry," said Coyote. "I know how we can do it. Just stand up straight and put your hands against the side of the well. Lift your head so your horns

stick out behind, and I'll climb
on your back. As soon as I'm
out, I'll reach over and pull
you up."

It sounded good to White
Beard. He did what he was told,
and Coyote climbed on top of
him. But then, when Coyote was
free, he ran around the edge of
the well, laughing at White
Beard. White Beard was furious.

"Friend," said Coyote, "if
your brain was as big as your
beard, you would have thought
about how to get out before you
jumped in."

*The truth hits hardest when
it's too late to complain.*

LOOK AHEAD

Ananse's
Feast
An Ashanti Tale

In *Ananse's
Feast,* find out
the big idea
behind why a spider and a
turtle trick each other.

Vocabulary

Words to Know

brilliant	**greedy**	**feast**
delighted	**guest**	**stomach**

Many words have more than one meaning. To decide which meaning is being used, look for clues in the sentence or paragraph around it.

Read the paragraph below. Pay attention to its meaning as a whole. Does *brilliant* mean "having great ability" or "sparkling"?

A Guest with Bad Manners!

Polly Peacock set the table for a <u>feast</u>. She put out food and cleaned the silverware until it was shining and <u>brilliant</u>. Polly was <u>delighted</u> to see her first dinner <u>guest</u>, Spinner the Spider. At least she was happy until she saw how <u>greedy</u> Spinner was. He ate and ate until his <u>stomach</u> was full and most of the food was gone. Next time, Polly would have her party when Spinner was on vacation!

Write About It

Write an invitation for Polly's next dinner party. Use as many vocabulary words as you can.

Ananse's Feast

An Ashanti Tale

retold by Tololwa M. Mollel • illustrated by Andrew Glass

The earth was hot and barren and no one had much to eat except Ananse the Spider. Before the drought clever Ananse had stored away food from his farm, and now he decided to treat himself to a feast.

Ananse shut his door and windows and sealed all the cracks in the walls of his old hut.

"I don't want the delicious smell of my cooking to bring hungry visitors," he muttered.

But somehow the aroma of food escaped and reached Akye the Turtle, who was searching for something to eat on a dusty riverbed nearby.

"I'll drop in on my old friend Ananse," thought hungry Akye. "I'm sure he'll spare me a bite."

Ananse was setting the table when he heard a knock on the door. He stood still and listened. "Whoever it is will soon go away," he thought hopefully.

The knocking didn't stop, however, and Ananse had to open the door. He didn't want to share his feast with anyone. Yet when he saw his friend Akye, he couldn't bring himself to send him away.

"Oh, it is you, Akye," said Ananse, smiling.
"Come in and be my guest!"

Akye stared at the mountain of food. He didn't
know where to start. "I'll eat the golden, crisp fried
plantain first," he thought. "How delicious it looks!
Oh, look at the steaming hot soft yam and the
pepper soup. No, I'll start on the fluffy coconut
rice and the creamy beans with ground peanuts."

He was reaching for the rice when Ananse
stopped him. "Your hands are dirty!" he told Akye.
"In my house, it is only good manners to wash
your hands before eating."

Akye looked at his hands, dusty and dirty from his manner of walking on all fours. "Can I have some water to wash them?" he asked.

"I'm sorry, I've used up all the water," replied Ananse. "You must go and wash your hands at the river."

The river was dry except for a few puddles. Akye washed his hands thoroughly in one of them. And back he crawled,

a-kye-kye-die
a-kye-kye-die,

his empty stomach moaning, *Oyei-yaai oyei-yaai!* as he thought of the fluffy coconut rice and the creamy beans with ground peanuts.

But greedy Ananse had eaten up the rice and the beans.

"No matter," thought Akye, "I'll have the steaming hot soft yam and the pepper—"

"Look, your hands, you didn't wash them," Ananse said, with a frown.

Akye looked at his dusty hands and shook his head. "Strange—I did wash them. Well, I'll go and wash them again."

At the river Akye rubbed, scrubbed, rinsed, and wiped his hands. Then up the riverbank he clambered,

 a-kye-kye-die
 a-kye-kye-die,

his empty stomach groaning, *Oyei-yai-yaai oyei-yai-yaai!* as he thought of the steaming hot soft yam and the pepper soup.

He got back to find selfish Ananse finishing up the yam and the soup.

"Your hands are still dirty!" mumbled Ananse.

"But I just washed them!" protested Akye.

"You don't seem to have done a good job of it," replied Ananse, laughing. "Go back to the river!"

By the time Akye returned from the river, cunning Ananse had eaten all the food and was wearing a big satisfied grin.

Akye suddenly realized how Ananse had tricked him. He only smiled, however, and said to well-fed Ananse, "Thank you for inviting me to the feast. I hope one day I can repay you."

A few days later, the drought ended. Rain came down. The earth bloomed and food crops burst forth. Rivers flowed, teeming with fish and crabs.

It rained so much that farms became swampy. The harvest was late, and Ananse, who was not a good fisherman, had little to eat. So he was delighted to receive an invitation to a feast at the turtle's home under the river.

Hungry Ananse arrived at the river dressed for the feast in a brilliant ceremonial robe. He climbed up a tall tree on the riverbank.

Then, straight as an arrow, he dived into the water.

Bul bul bul bul bul, he sank.

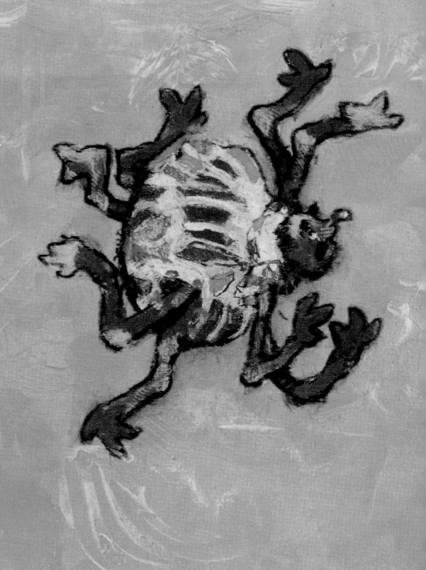

He was too light to stay underwater, though.
And *bul bul bul bul bul*, he rose, floating
back to the surface.
He climbed higher on the tree and dived again.
Bul bul bul bul bul, he sank.
Bul bul bul bul bul, he rose.

Then Ananse had an idea. "I know how I can get to the feast!" he exclaimed. He filled the enormous pockets of his robe with pebbles from the beach. Then he climbed to the very top of the tree and came streaking down.

Bul bul bul bul bul, he sank.

Bul bul bul bul bul, he sank.

Down to the feast!

Akye was seated at a table laden with plump mounds of juicy, tender crabmeat, dressed in a brilliant ceremonial robe of his own. With his heavy shell, he had no trouble staying down.

The turtle noticed the bulging weight of pebbles in Ananse's pockets and touched the spider's robe admiringly.

"What a beautiful robe!" he said, and smiled. "But I suggest you take it off before we eat."

"What!" cried Ananse.

"In my house," Akye said sweetly, "it is only good manners to take off your robe before eating." And he began to slip out of his own robe.

Ananse couldn't let Akye think he was an ill-mannered guest. Reluctantly, he took off his robe. And although he tried hard to cling to the table . . .

Bul bul bul bul bul, he rose.

Bul bul bul bul bul, he rose.

Back to the surface!

Unable to return to the feast without his heavy robe, Ananse sat shivering on the bank, his empty stomach wailing,

Oyei-yai-yai-yaai!

Oyei-yai-yai-yaai!

as he thought of the plump mounds of juicy, tender crabmeat.

Some time later, well-fed Akye walked out of
the river,

a-kye-kye-die
a-kye-kye-die.

With a big satisfied grin, he came to squat
alongside his old friend Ananse.

"What a delicious feast that was," said Akye,
rubbing his full belly with pleasure. "Thank you
so much for coming. The meal would not have
been the same without you. Let's make sure we
have another feast soon!"

Tololwa M. Mollel

Tololwa M. Mollel grew up in Tanzania, a country in East Africa. He lived with his grandparents, who were storytellers. He not only loved hearing their stories, he loved to read other people's stories—and to write his own. "I wrote about pirates, magical lamps, knights, and detectives at various stages of my school years," he says.

When Mr. Mollel went to college in Canada, he kept writing for fun. After he married and had a child, he decided that he wanted to write for children. What would he write about? Since he knew so many African folk tales from his childhood, he decided to use a story that had been told to him by his grandfather. Mr. Mollel called it *The Orphan Boy*. In this Masai folk tale, a boy learns about secrets, trust, and betrayal. Mr. Mollel has retold other folk tales from different parts of Africa. His stories often have a lesson about life in them.

"Writing for children for me is both challenging and rewarding," he says. "It is challenging to put complicated ideas into simple terms. It is rewarding when children enjoy the stories."

Reader Response

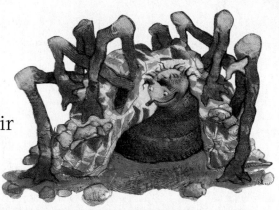

Open for Discussion

People tell this tale to their children. Why do you think they do?

Comprehension Check

1. Which character is more clever—Ananse or Akye? Give examples from the story to support your answer.

2. Think of two or three words to describe Ananse. Find parts of the story that support your choices.

3. Will Ananse and Akye ever have another meal together? Why or why not? Use details from the story to support your answer.

4. What is one big idea, or **theme,** in *Ananse's Feast*? (Theme)

5. In what way can this **theme** help you in your life? (Theme)

 Test Prep

Look Back and Write

Look back through the story. How are Ananse and Akye alike? How are they different? Use details from the story to explain.

Literature Connection

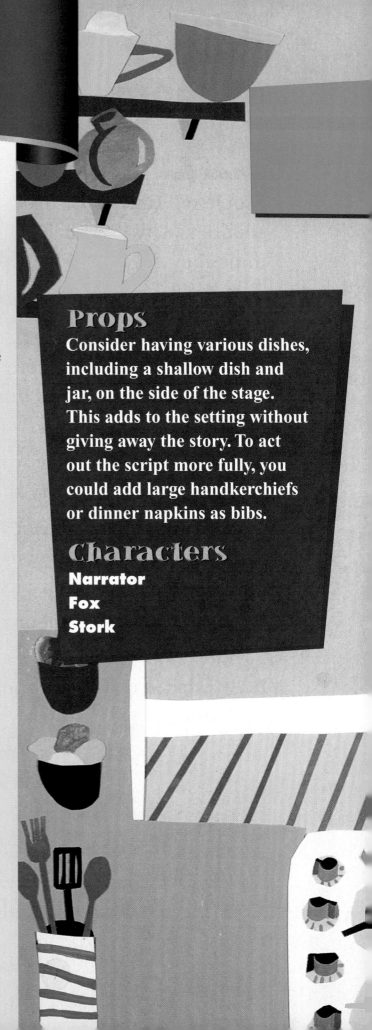

 **Test Prep**

How to Read a Fable

1. Preview

- A fable is a short story that often teaches a lesson. Notice that this fable is written as a play. Who are the characters in the play? What kind of information do you find under *Props?*

2. Read and List Events

- Read the play to find out what happens in the beginning, middle, and end. Keep track of the story events. What is the lesson at the end?

3. Think and Connect

Think about *Ananse's Feast.* Then look over your notes from "The Fox and the Stork."

Could the lesson at the end of "The Fox and the Stork" be the lesson of *Ananse's Feast* as well? Why or why not?

Props

Consider having various dishes, including a shallow dish and jar, on the side of the stage. This adds to the setting without giving away the story. To act out the script more fully, you could add large handkerchiefs or dinner napkins as bibs.

Characters

Narrator

Fox

Stork

The FOX and the Stork

retold by Suzanne I. Barchers

Narrator: There was a time when the fox and the stork were very good friends. They enjoyed talking about their days. One day they decided to share a meal together.

Fox: Why don't you come to dinner, my good friend? I'll fix my best soup!

Stork: That sounds fine! When shall I come?

Fox: Tonight would be fine for me.

Narrator: That night, the stork was happy just thinking about a bowl of good soup. She even arrived a little early at the fox's den.

Fox: Hello, my friend. Let's waste no time. The soup is ready.

Narrator: But the stork had quite a surprise. The soup was in a shallow bowl. She couldn't eat any of it with her long beak.

Stork: My beak is much too long to be able to eat from that bowl, Fox.

Fox: I *am* sorry that you don't like my soup.

Narrator: And so the stork went home hungry. But the next day she invited the fox to dinner.

Stork: Fox, let's forget that I went home hungry last night. Why don't you come to my home for dinner tonight?

Fox: It would be my pleasure.

Narrator: That night the fox showed up at the stork's home, eager for another meal.

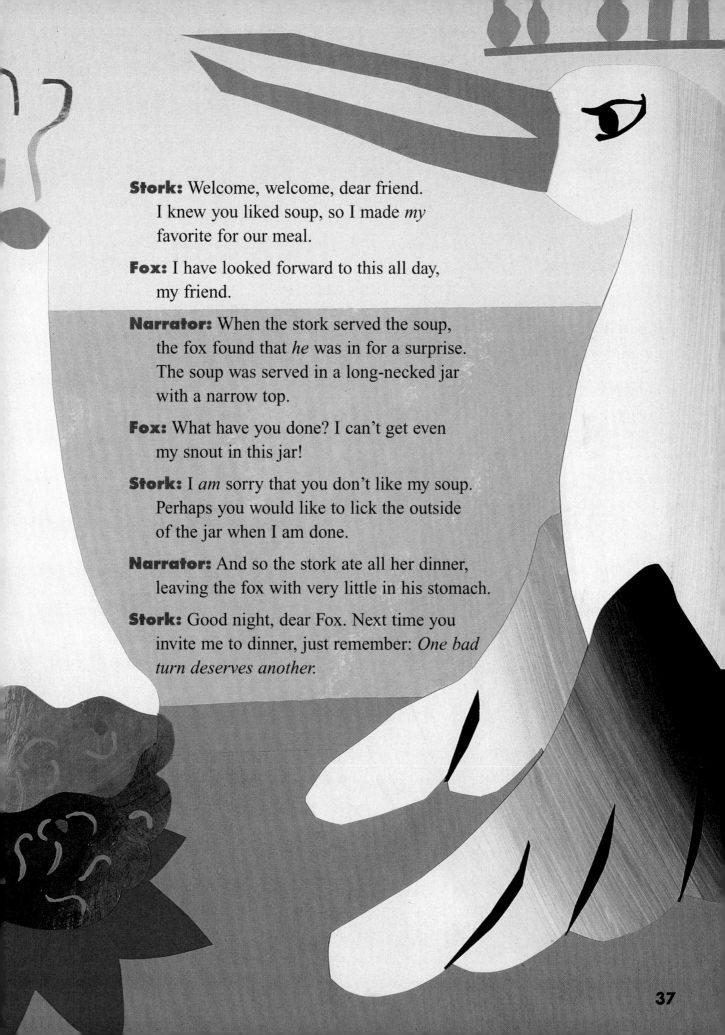

Stork: Welcome, welcome, dear friend. I knew you liked soup, so I made *my* favorite for our meal.

Fox: I have looked forward to this all day, my friend.

Narrator: When the stork served the soup, the fox found that *he* was in for a surprise. The soup was served in a long-necked jar with a narrow top.

Fox: What have you done? I can't get even my snout in this jar!

Stork: I *am* sorry that you don't like my soup. Perhaps you would like to lick the outside of the jar when I am done.

Narrator: And so the stork ate all her dinner, leaving the fox with very little in his stomach.

Stork: Good night, dear Fox. Next time you invite me to dinner, just remember: *One bad turn deserves another.*

Setting

- The **setting** is the time and place in which a story happens.

- Look for details or clues that tell you when and where a story takes place.

- Understanding the setting can sometimes help you understand a character's actions.

Read "A Hike with Dad" from *The Lost Lake* by Allen Say.

Write About It

1. Make a list of the words that help you see the setting in "A Hike with Dad."

2. Pretend you are with Dad too. Write a diary entry describing the setting. Share your diary entry with a classmate.

A Hike with Dad

by Allen Say

We started early in the morning. When the fog cleared we saw other hikers ahead of us. Sure enough, Dad became very glum.

"We're going cross-country, partner," he said.

"Won't we get lost?"

"A wise man never leaves home without his compass."

So we went off the trail. The hills went on and on. The mountains went on and on. It was kind of lonesome. It seemed as if Dad and I were the only people left in the world.

And then we hiked into a big forest.

At noontime we stopped by a creek and ate lunch and drank ice-cold water straight from the stream. I threw

rocks in the water and fish, like shadows, darted in pools.

"Isn't this a good place to camp, Dad?"

"I thought we were looking for our lake."

"Yes, right . . ." I mumbled.

The forest went on and on.

"I don't mean to scare you, Son," Dad said. "But we're in bear country. We don't want to surprise them so we have to make a lot of noise. If they hear us, they'll just go away."

What a time to tell me! I started to shout as loudly as I could. Even Dad wouldn't be able to beat off bears. I thought about those people having fun back at the lake. I thought about the creek, too, with all those fish in it. That would have been a fine place to camp.

In *Sam and the Lucky Money*, Sam is out with his mother on Chinese New Year's Day. Read and think about how the setting helps determine what Sam does with his lucky money.

Vocabulary

Words to Know

appreciate	rustling	scolded
dragon	lucky	startled

When you read, you may come across a word you don't know. To figure out the unfamiliar word, look for clues around it. A clue might be found in an explanation given before or after the unknown word.

Read the paragraph below. Notice how an explanation of *lucky* helps you understand what it means.

The Perfect Present

"I need a gift Grandma can <u>appreciate</u>," Felicia said. She <u>scolded</u> herself for spending her money on candy. A noise <u>startled</u> her—Grandpa! He said, "Here's my <u>lucky</u> coin. Touch it for good fortune." There was a soft <u>rustling</u> as Grandpa took the coin from his pocket. On it was a picture of a <u>dragon</u>. An idea came to her as Felicia touched the coin. She'd write Grandma a story!

Write About It

What story could Felicia tell? Use vocabulary words to write her story.

Sam and the Lucky Money

by Karen Chinn
illustrated by Cornelius Van Wright
and Ying-Hwa Hu

Sam could hardly wait to get going. He zipped up his jacket and patted his pockets. It was time to go to Chinatown for New Year's Day!

Sam thought about sweet oranges and "lucky money": Crisp dollar bills tucked in small red envelopes called *leisees*.

Sam's grandparents gave him leisees every New Year. Each envelope was decorated with a symbol of luck: Two golden mandarins. A Chinese junk. A slithering dragon. A giant peach. Sam's leisees were embossed in gold.

Sam counted out four dollars. Boy, did he feel rich! His parents said he didn't have to buy a notebook or socks as usual. This year he could spend his lucky money *his* way.

"Sam!" his mother called. "It's time to go shopping. Hurry, so we don't miss the lion!"

"Coming!" said Sam.

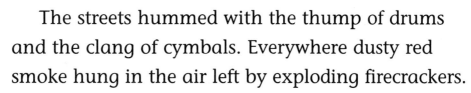

The streets hummed with the thump of drums and the clang of cymbals. Everywhere dusty red smoke hung in the air left by exploding firecrackers.

"Give me your hand," said his mother. "I don't want you to get lost." Sam took her hand reluctantly. It seemed like everyone was shopping for New Year's meals. There were so many people crowded around the overflowing vegetable bins that Sam had to look out for elbows and shopping bags.

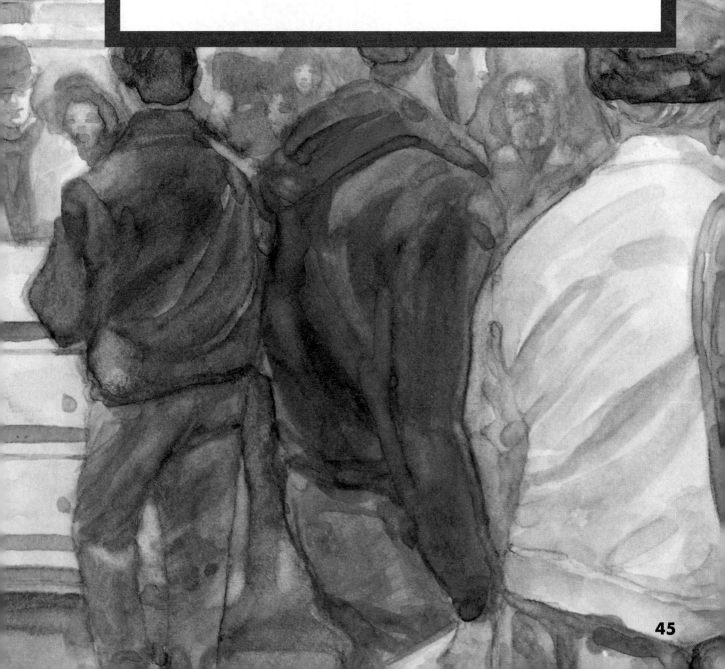

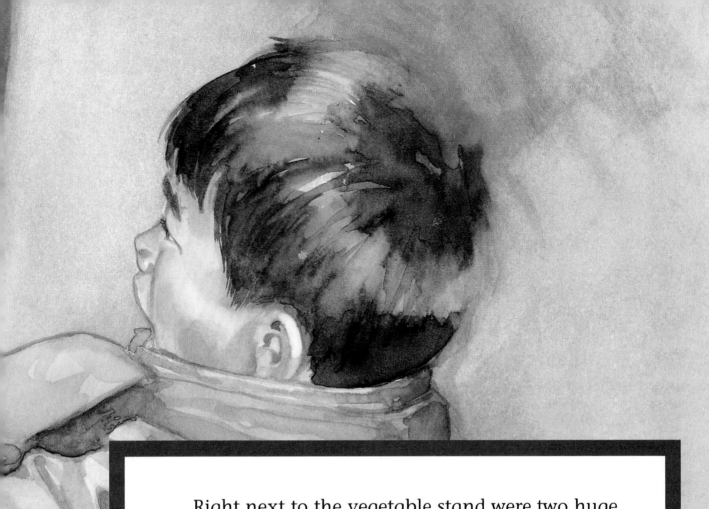

Right next to the vegetable stand were two huge red-paper mounds. Sam kicked the piles with his right foot, and then with his left foot, until he created a small blizzard. On his third kick he felt his foot land on something strange.

"Aiya!" someone cried out in pain.

Startled, he looked up to find an old man sitting against the wall. The stranger was rubbing his foot. *Bare feet in winter!* Sam thought. *Where are his shoes?*

Sam stared at the man's dirty clothes as he backed away. He found his mother picking out oranges and he tugged on her sleeve, pulling harder than he meant to.

"Hey, I need this arm," she said. "Where have you been? It's time to go."

For once, Sam was glad to follow his mother.

In the bakery window, Sam eyed a gleaming row of fresh *char siu bao*, his favorite honey-topped buns. When they opened the door, the smell of sweet egg tarts and coconut pastries erased any thought of the stranger. Sam wondered how many sweets he could buy with four dollars.

"*Nay yu mat yeh ah*?" said a young woman from behind the counter. When Sam gave her a puzzled look, she repeated the question in English. "What do you want?"

Sam was about to ask for buns when he noticed a tray full of New Year's cookies. They were shaped like fish, with fat, pleated tails that looked like little toes. He couldn't help but think about the old man again. Sam decided he wasn't hungry after all. Suddenly, he heard a noise from outside that sounded like a thousand leaves rustling. He ran to the window to see what was happening.

"Look!" he yelled. Bundles of firecrackers were exploding in the street. Rounding the corner was the festival lion, followed by a band of cymbals and drums. Sam pulled his mother outside.

The colorful lion wove down the street like a giant centipede. Teased by a clown wearing a round mask, it tossed its head up and down.

It came to a halt in front of a meat market, and sniffed a giant leisee that hung in the doorway, along with a bouquet of lettuce leaves. With loud fanfare, the band urged the lion toward its prize.

"Take the food! Take the money! Bring us good luck for the New Year!" Sam shouted along with the others. His heart pounded in time with the drum's beat. With a sudden lunge, the lion devoured the leisee all in an eye-blink and continued down the street. The crowd clapped and then quickly dispersed.

"That was a hungry lion," Sam's mother joked. Now he felt hungry too, and wanted to go back to the bakery.

But just then, a large "Grand Opening" sign caught Sam's eye. In the window were cars, planes, robots, and stuffed animals. A new toy store! Just the place to spend his lucky money!

Sam ran down one aisle, then another. He examined a police car with a wailing siren and flashing lights. He squeezed a talking pig and laughed at its loud "Oink, oink!" Then, he spotted the basketballs.

A new basketball was the perfect way to spend his lucky money. But when he saw the price tag, he got angry.

"I only have four dollars," he shouted. "I can't buy this." In fact, everything he touched cost more than that.

"What is four dollars good for?" he complained, stamping his feet. His mother scrunched up her eyes, the way she always did when she scolded him, and guided him out the door.

Sam couldn't help it. Even with all the shiny gold on them, the leisees seemed worthless.

"Sam, when someone gives you something, you should appreciate it," his mother said as she marched him along. Sam stuffed his leisees back in his pockets. The sun had disappeared behind some clouds, and he was starting to feel the chill. He dragged his feet along the sidewalk.

Suddenly, Sam saw a pair of bare feet, and instantly recognized them. They belonged to the old man he had seen earlier. The man also remembered him, and smiled. Sam froze in his steps, staring at the man's feet.

His mother kept walking. When she turned back to check on Sam, she noticed the old man. "Oh," she said, shifting her shopping bags so she could dig in her purse for some coins. "Sorry—I only have a quarter." The man bowed his head several times in thanks.

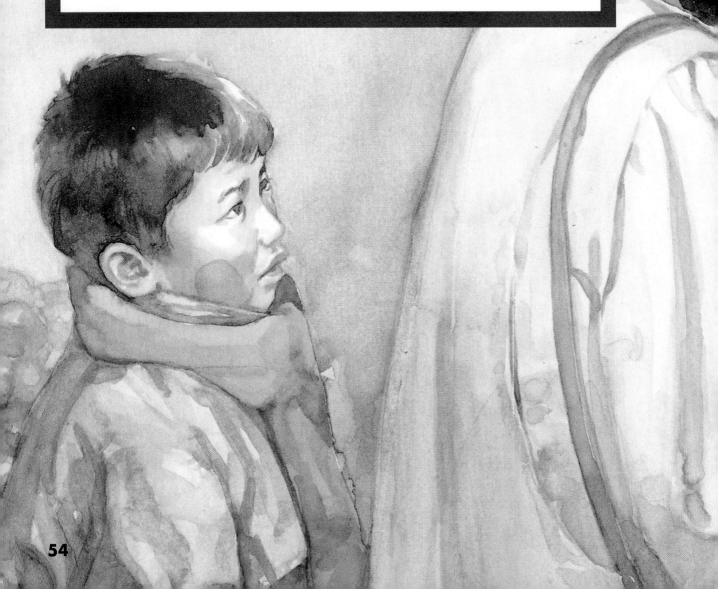

He acts like it's a million bucks, Sam thought, shaking his head. As they started to walk away, Sam looked down at his own feet, warm and dry in his boots. Suddenly he stopped.

"Can I really do anything I want with my lucky money?" he asked.

"Yes, of course," his mother answered.

Sam pulled his leisees from his pockets. The golden dragon looked shinier than ever. He ran back and thrust his lucky money into the surprised man's hands.

"You can't buy shoes with this," he told the man, "but I know you can buy some socks." The stranger laughed, and so did Sam's mother.

Sam walked back to his mother and took her warm hand. She smiled and gave a gentle squeeze. And as they headed home for more New Year's celebration, Sam knew he was the lucky one.

About the Author
Karen Chinn

Karen Chinn likes to write stories that bring different cultures together. When Karen Chinn was growing up in Seattle, Washington, there weren't many books about Asian Americans in modern settings. She wrote *Sam and the Lucky Money* to celebrate Asian American culture. "I wanted to capture some of the rituals and customs of Chinese New Year's, as well as the excitement of it," she has said. Mrs. Chinn and her husband currently live in Seattle with their daughter.

About the Illustrators
Cornelius Van Wright and Ying-Hwa Hu

Cornelius Van Wright and Ying-Hwa Hu have worked as a team to illustrate two other award-winning books, *Zora Hurston and the Chinaberry Tree* and *A House by the River*. They used watercolors to paint the pictures for these books, as well as for *Sam and the Lucky Money*.

Reader Response

Open for Discussion

If you met Sam, what would you ask him about himself and where he lives?

Comprehension Check

1. Did Sam do the right thing when he gave his money to the man? Use details to support your answer.

2. Sam's mood changes often in this story. Choose a page and tell what his mood is. Tell why he feels as he does.

3. Look back at all of Sam's choices. What do you think Sam will do with his leisees next New Year? Why?

4. What is the **setting** of *Sam and the Lucky Money?* (Setting)

5. How would the story be different if the **setting** were in a hot place or during the summer? (Setting)

 Test Prep

Look Back and Write

Look back at pages 47–51. The author uses vivid details. Write how the author describes the red paper, the fish tails, the noise Sam hears outside the bakery, and the lion.

What to Do with Money

by Benjamin Elkin

One thing you can do with money, of course, is to spend it. You can use it to buy things you need or want.

But suppose you have some money that you don't want to spend—at least not right away. What can you do with it?

You could hide it under your mattress. Or you could put it in a can and bury it in your backyard.

But those aren't very safe things to do. So people have found better ways of taking care of the money they don't want to spend.

Sometimes they lend that money to the government or to a business. The people they lend it to pay them interest. Interest is money people are paid for letting someone else borrow their money. It's a little like getting paid rent for letting someone else use your house.

Sometimes people buy part of a business with their money. Each part they buy is called "a share of stock." As long as they keep those stocks, they will get part of any money the business makes. When they want their money back, they can sell their stocks.

Many people put money in savings accounts at a bank. The bank works with this money. People can borrow it to build a house or a factory. They can borrow it to run a farm or get a new car.

You can put money into savings accounts too. It doesn't take a lot of money to open one.

The people who borrow the money pay the bank interest. Then the bank pays the people with savings accounts part of that interest.

Many people also put money into checking accounts at banks. They know their money is safe there.

Then, when they want to pay a bill or buy something, they write a check for the amount of money they need.

A check is a specially printed piece of paper. The person who fills it out writes down how much money should be paid and to whom. Then the person signs his or her own name. The person being paid can take the check to a bank and get money for it.

There are many ways to use money. Some are wise and some are foolish. Until you know a lot about money, it is a good idea to ask an adult to help you figure out how to use yours.

If you start saving just 50 cents a school day in this grade . . .	you'll have this amount at high school graduation*
3rd grade	$900
4th grade	$810
5th grade	$720
6th grade	$630
7th grade	$540
8th grade	$450
9th grade	$360

*Based on 180 school days in each year × 50 cents a day = $90 a school year

Cause and Effect

- A **cause** is why something happens.

- An **effect** is what happens.

- Sometimes an author uses clue words, such as *so* and *because,* to tell what happens and why.

- When clue words are not present to signal cause and effect, look for what happens. Stop and think why it happens.

Read "Fire!" by Caroline Evans from *Ranger Rick* magazine.

Talk About It

1. What happened to the pine tree? Why?

2. What effects might the forest fire have on camping and hiking in the forest?

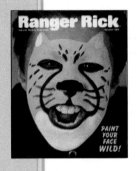

by Caroline Evans

Imagine a hot summer day in a forest in the western United States. A mighty thunderstorm turns the blue sky black. Zap! A bolt of lightning streaks toward the ground and strikes the top of a tall pine tree. Electric current zips down through its trunk and roots. In an instant, the pine tree explodes into a flaming torch.

The burning branches pop and scatter onto the forest floor. Fire spreads to dry twigs and needles. Flames dance over dead logs and leap up nearby tree

trunks. Soon the forest crackles and snaps in a red-orange light.

This is the end of the forest, right? Actually, the answer is bigger than that. A fire can be just another step in the forest's ongoing natural cycle.

LOOK AHEAD

In *Thunder Cake,* a young girl is afraid of thunder. Read and find out the effects of her grandmother's cure.

Vocabulary

Words to Know

distance   thunder   lightning
measured   weather   recipe

As you read, you may come across
a word you don't know. To figure
out its meaning, look for clues
around it. A clue might be in an
explanation or definition given
before or after the word.

Notice how *recipe* is used in
the paragraph below. Find an
explanation in the sentences
around it.

Calm During the Storm

The weather was different today. The sky
was a dark mass of clouds and the wind was
still. In the distance, Sami could see bright
flashes of lightning. Sami's sister Liz was afraid
of storms, so Sami got out a recipe for cookies.
As they followed the directions and measured
the sugar and flour, they could hear loud booms
of thunder. But Liz was having fun—she wasn't
scared anymore.

Talk About It

Tell about weather that scares you.
Use some vocabulary words.

Thunder Cake

written and illustrated by Patricia Polacco

Grandma looked at the horizon, drew a deep breath and said, "This is Thunder Cake baking weather, all right. Looks like a storm coming to me."

"Child, you come out from under that bed. It's only thunder you're hearing," my grandma said.

The air was hot, heavy, and damp. A loud clap of thunder shook the house, rattled the windows, and made me grab her close.

"Steady, child," she cooed. "Unless you let go of me, we won't be able to make a Thunder Cake today!"

"Thunder Cake?" I stammered as I hugged her even closer.

"Don't pay attention to that old thunder, except to see how close the storm is getting. When you see the lightning, start counting . . . real slow. When you hear the thunder, stop counting. That number is how many miles away the storm is. Understand?" she asked. "We need to know how far away the storm is, so we have time to make the cake and get it into the oven before the storm comes, or it won't be real Thunder Cake."

Her eyes surveyed the black clouds a way off in the distance. Then she strode into the kitchen. Her worn hands pulled a thick book from the shelf above the woodstove.

"Let's find that recipe, child," she crowed as she lovingly fingered the grease-stained pages to a creased spot.

"Here it is . . . Thunder Cake!"

She carefully penned the ingredients on a piece of notepaper. "Now let's gather all the things we'll need!" she exclaimed as she scurried toward the back door.

We were by the barn door when a huge bolt of lightning flashed. I started counting, like Grandma told me to, "1-2-3-4-5-6-7-8-9-10."

Then the thunder ROARED!

"Ten miles . . . it's ten miles away," Grandma said as she looked at the sky. "About an hour away, I'd say. You'll have to hurry, child. Gather them eggs careful-like," she said.

Eggs from mean old Nellie Peck Hen. I was scared. I knew she would try to peck me.

"I'm here, she won't hurt you. Just get them eggs," Grandma said softly.

The lightning flashed again. "1-2-3-4-5-6-7-8-9,"
I counted.

"Nine miles," Grandma reminded me.

Milk was next. Milk from old Kick Cow. As
Grandma milked her, Kick Cow turned and looked
mean, right at me. I was scared. She looked so big.

ZIP, went the lightning. "1-2-3-4-5-6-7-8," I
counted.

BAROOOOOOOOM, went the thunder.

"Eight miles, child," Grandma croaked. "Now we
have to get chocolate and sugar, and flour from the
dry shed."

I was scared as we walked down the path from the farmhouse through Tangleweed Woods to the dry shed. Suddenly the lightning slit the sky!

"1-2-3-4-5-6-7," I counted.

BOOOOOOM BA-BOOOOOOM, crashed the thunder. It scared me a lot, but I kept walking with Grandma.

Another jagged edge of lightning flashed as I crept into the dry shed! "1-2-3-4-5-6," I counted.

CRACKLE, CRACKLE BOOOOOOOM, KA-BOOOOOM, the thunder bellowed. It was dark and I was scared.

"I'm here, child," Grandma said softly from the doorway. "Hurry now, we haven't got much time. We've got everything but the secret ingredient."

"Three overripe tomatoes and some strawberries," Grandma whispered as she squinted at the list.

I climbed up high on the trellis. The ground looked a long way down. I was scared.

"I'm here, child," she said. Her voice was steady and soft. "You won't fall."

I reached three luscious tomatoes while she picked strawberries. Lightning again!

"1-2-3-4-5," I counted.

KA-BANG BOOOOOOOOOAROOOOM, the thunder growled.

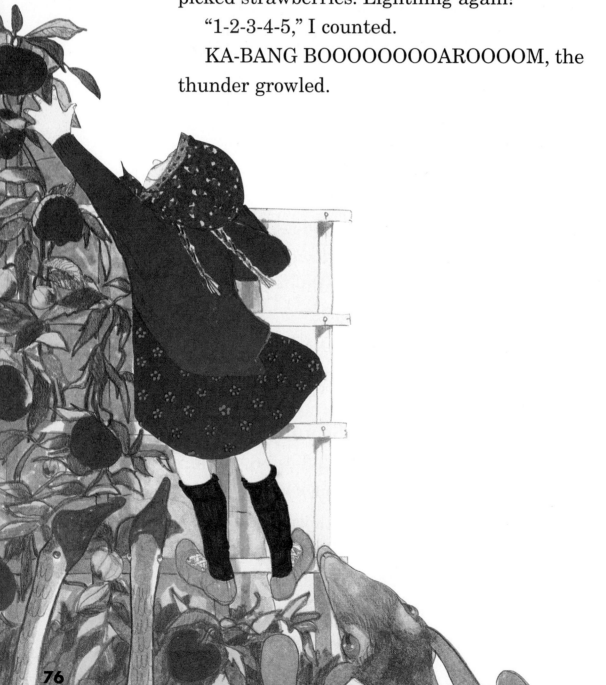

We hurried back to the house and the warm
kitchen, and we measured the ingredients. I poured
them into the mixing bowl while Grandma mixed.
I churned butter for the frosting and melted
chocolate. Finally, we poured the batter into the
cake pans and put them into the oven together.

Lightning lit the kitchen! I only counted to
three and the thunder RRRRUMBLED and
CRASHED.

"Three miles away," Grandma said, "and the
cake is in the oven. We made it! We'll have a real
Thunder Cake!"

As we waited for the cake, Grandma looked out the window for a long time. "Why, you aren't afraid of thunder. You're too brave!" she said as she looked right at me.

"I'm not brave, Grandma," I said. "I was under the bed! Remember?"

"But you got out from under it," she answered, "and you got eggs from mean old Nellie Peck Hen, you got milk from old Kick Cow, you went through Tangleweed Woods to the dry shed, you climbed the trellis in the barnyard. From where I sit, only a very brave person could have done all them things!"

I thought and thought as the storm rumbled closer. She was right. I was brave!

"Brave people can't be afraid of a sound, child," she said as we spread out the tablecloth and set the table. When we were done, we hurried into the kitchen to take the cake out of the oven. After the cake had cooled, we frosted it.

Just then the lightning flashed, and this time it lit the whole sky.

Even before the last flash had faded, the
thunder ROLLED, BOOOOOMED, CRASHED, and
BBBBAAAAARRRRROOOOOOOOMMMMMMM-
MMMED just above us. The storm was here!

"Perfect," Grandma cooed, "just perfect." She
beamed as she added the last strawberry to
the glistening chocolate frosting on top of our
Thunder Cake.

As rain poured down on our roof, Grandma cut a wedge for each of us. She poured us steaming cups of tea from the samovar.

When the thunder ROARED above us so hard it shook the windows and rattled the dishes in the cupboards, we just smiled and ate our Thunder Cake.

From that time on, I never feared the voice of thunder again.

Patricia Polacco

Patricia Polacco comes from a long line of storytellers. "My fondest memories are of sitting around a stove or open fire," she remembers, "eating apples and popping popcorn while

listening to the old ones tell glorious stories about the past." Many of her relatives came from Russia. As a child, Ms. Polacco learned of Russian traditions and folk tales through these stories.

Along with *Thunder Cake,* Ms. Polacco has written and illustrated other stories about her family. *The Trees of the Dancing Goats* also takes place on her Babushka's (Grandma's) farm in Michigan. Ms. Polacco's story *Uncle Vova's Tree* is a holiday tale about traditions that her relatives brought to America from Russia.

Ms. Polacco is an expert on Russian paintings and has studied art in both the United States and Australia. She now lives in Oakland, California.

Reader Response

Open for Discussion

If you were with someone who was afraid of a storm, what would you do to help that person get over the fear?

Comprehension Check

1. Look back through the story. Why did Grandma make a Thunder Cake?

2. Does the girl visiting her grandmother live on a farm herself? How can you tell? Use details from the story to support your answer.

3. Thunder can be frightening because it is so loud. Look through the story. What are some of the many ways that the author describes the sound thunder makes?

4. What is the **cause** and what is the **effect** in this sentence? *The girl was afraid of Nellie Peck Hen because she thought the hen would peck her.* (Cause and Effect)

5. What is the **cause** and what are the **effects** in this sentence from the story? *A loud clap of thunder shook the house, rattled the windows, and made me grab her close.* (Cause and Effect)

Test Prep
Look Back and Write

Look back through the story. What does the girl do from the time she starts counting to the time the thunder is right above the house?

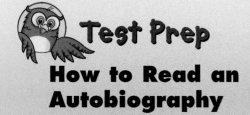

Test Prep

How to Read an Autobiography

1. Preview

- In an autobiography, the author tells about his or her life. Look at the pictures. What do you notice about the kinds of pictures the author uses?

2. Read and Take Notes

- Read to find out about Patricia Polacco's life. List the important childhood experiences she writes about. Remember that your information will come from different places in the selection.

3. Think and Connect

Think about *Thunder Cake.* Then look over your notes on *Firetalking.*

What experiences in Patricia Polacco's life might have helped her write *Thunder Cake?*

by Patricia Polacco

My mother's people were Russian and my father's people were Irish. In *The Keeping Quilt,* I tell how my mother's family came to be here in America. I still use this same wonderful quilt for wedding chuppas, tablecloths for special occasions, and to welcome new babies into the world. Both sets of my grandparents were captivating storytellers. With almost no urging at all they squinted up their eyes, watched our faces, and began to "tell."

Many of our evenings were spent in front of the fireplace, popping corn, eating apple wedges, and hearing rich, incredible tales. My babushka

Firetalking

(my Ukrainian grandmother) called this "firetalking." Whenever she finished one of her tales of magic and mystery, my brother and I would always ask, "Bubby, is that a true story?" She would look at us and reply, "Of course it's true . . . but it may not have happened."

In both Mom's house and at Dad's place there was always a rocking chair, just for me. I spent hours and hours just rocking and dreaming every day. I spent a lot of time in my imagination. It soothed the pain of not doing well in school.

I had difficulty reading. Math was and still is almost impossible for me. I knew that inside I was very smart, but at school I felt stupid and slow. I had to work very hard to learn things. Now that I am grown up I realize that I process information differently than most people do. My brain scrambles images that my eyes see. But once I got the hang of it, I went on in school. I even ended up graduating from college, and getting my Ph.D. in Art History.

Skill Lesson

Compare and Contrast

- We **compare** when we say how things are alike.

- We **contrast** when we say how things are different.

- Clue words, such as *yet* and *however,* can signal a comparison or a contrast.

Read "Afraid of the Dark" from *Darkness and the Butterfly* by Ann Grifalconi.

Write About It

1. Fold a sheet of paper in half the long way. Write *day* at the top left of the paper and *night* at the top right of the paper. Under the correct word, write words or phrases from the selection that compare how Osa acts during the day and at night.

2. Compare and contrast your findings with classmates.

Afraid of the Dark
by Ann Grifalconi

There was a bright and pretty girl named Osa who was *so* afraid of the dark, no matter what her mother or grandfather said when evening came Osa would not leave the house. She would sit in the corner hugging her knees to her chin and her eyes would grow big and black with fear.

And she would stay that way refusing food and comfort 'til she fell asleep. Then her mother would lift her gently and tuck her into bed wishing she would find some way to show Osa not to fear—but to

know the beauties of the night.

Yet during the day, Osa was afraid of nothing she could see. For while Osa was very small, she was, oh, so lively. She could climb anything THREE TIMES her size, even the big Baobab Tree!

Osa was very curious too. And each day, she spent hours exploring every part of the valley where they lived. She loved to bring home the special things she found: some pretty wildflowers for her mother, a bright leaf or bird's feather for her grandfather. Or just some colored stones to keep.

But when nighttime fell, fearless daytime Osa became just as fearful as before.

LOOK AHEAD

In *One Grain of Rice*, Rani shows no fear of the raja and teaches him about sharing. Read to see how Rani and the raja are alike and different.

Vocabulary

Words to Know

double	reward	single
grain	palace	thief

When you read, you may come across a word you don't know. To figure out its meaning, look for clues near it. A clue might be found in an explanation given before or after the unknown word.

Read the paragraph below. Notice clues that explain what a *thief* is and does.

The Kind King

A <u>thief</u> stole jewels from the king's <u>palace</u>. The king said he would <u>reward</u> the person who caught the thief. A man said to the king, "I am the robber. I stole because my family doesn't have a <u>single</u> <u>grain</u> of oats or rice to eat." The king said, "If this is true, I will give you a job." The man thanked him and worked to pay back <u>double</u> what he stole.

Write About It

Imagine you are the thief. Write a brief thank-you note to the king. Use vocabulary words.

One Grain of Rice

BY *Demi*

A MATHEMATICAL FOLKTALE

Long ago in India, there lived a raja who believed that he was wise and fair, as a raja should be.

The people in his province were rice farmers. The raja decreed that everyone must give nearly all of their rice to him.

"I will store the rice safely," the raja promised the people, "so that in time of famine, everyone will have rice to eat, and no one will go hungry."

Each year, the raja's rice collectors gathered nearly all of the people's rice and carried it away to the royal storehouses.

For many years, the rice grew well. The people gave nearly all of their rice to the raja, and the storehouses were always full. But the people were left with only just enough rice to get by.

Then one year the rice grew badly, and there was famine and hunger. The people had no rice to give to the raja, and they had no rice to eat.

The raja's ministers implored him, "Your Highness, let us open the royal storehouses and give the rice to the people, as you promised."

"No!" cried the raja. "How do I know how long the famine may last? I must have the rice for myself. Promise or no promise, a raja must not go hungry!"

Time went on, and the people grew more and more hungry. But the raja would not give out the rice.

One day, the raja ordered a feast for himself and his court— as, it seemed to him, a raja should now and then, even when there is famine.

A servant led an elephant from a royal storehouse to the palace, carrying two full baskets of rice.

A village girl named Rani saw that a trickle of rice was falling from one of the baskets. Quickly she jumped up and walked along beside the elephant, catching the falling rice in her skirt. She was clever, and she began to make a plan.

At the palace, a guard cried, "Halt, thief! Where are you going with that rice?"

"I am not a thief," Rani replied. "This rice fell from one of the baskets, and I am returning it now to the raja."

When the raja heard about Rani's good deed, he asked his ministers to bring her before him.

"I wish to reward you for returning what belongs to me," the raja said to Rani. "Ask me for anything, and you shall have it."

"Your Highness," said Rani, "I do not deserve any reward at all. But if you wish, you may give me one grain of rice."

"Only one grain of rice?" exclaimed the raja. "Surely you will allow me to reward you more plentifully, as a raja should."

"Very well," said Rani. "If it pleases Your Highness, you may reward me in this way. Today, you will give me a single grain of rice. Then, each day for thirty days you will give me double the rice you gave me the day before. Thus, tomorrow you will give me two grains of rice, the next day four grains of rice, and so on for thirty days."

"This seems still to be a modest reward," said the raja. "But you shall have it."

And Rani was presented with a single grain of rice.

The next day, Rani was presented with two grains of rice.

And the following day, Rani was presented with four grains of rice.

On the ninth day, Rani was presented with two hundred and fifty-six grains of rice. She had received in all five hundred and eleven grains of rice, only enough for a small handful.

"This girl is honest, but not very clever," thought the raja. "She would have gained more rice by keeping what fell into her skirt!"

On the twelfth day, Rani received two thousand and forty-eight grains of rice, about four handfuls. On the thirteenth day, she received four thousand and ninety-six grains of rice, enough to fill a bowl.

On the sixteenth day, Rani was presented with a bag containing thirty-two thousand, seven hundred and sixty-eight grains of rice. All together she had enough rice for two full bags.

"This doubling adds up to more rice than I expected!" thought the raja. "But surely her reward won't amount to much more."

On the twentieth day, Rani was presented with sixteen more bags filled with rice.

On the twenty-first day, she received one million, forty-eight thousand, five hundred and seventy-six grains of rice, enough to fill a basket.

On the twenty-fourth day, Rani was presented with eight million, three hundred and eighty-eight thousand, six hundred and eight grains of rice—enough to fill eight baskets, which were carried to her by eight royal deer.

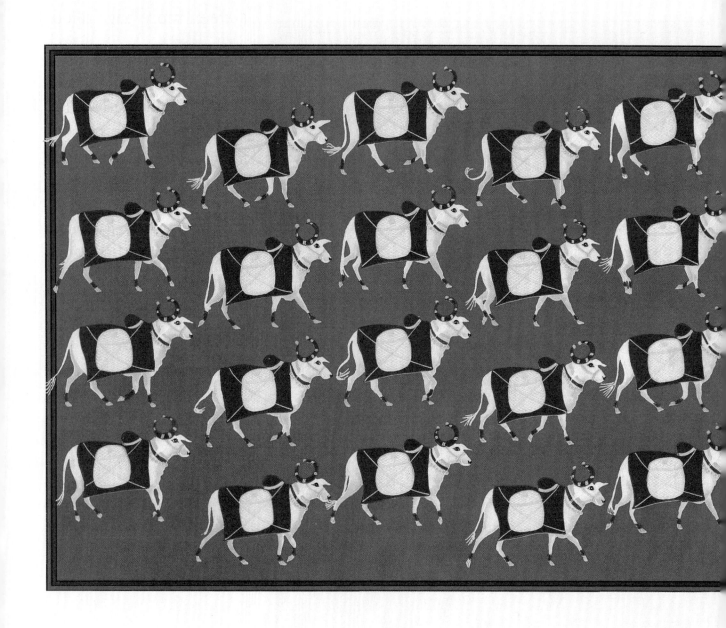

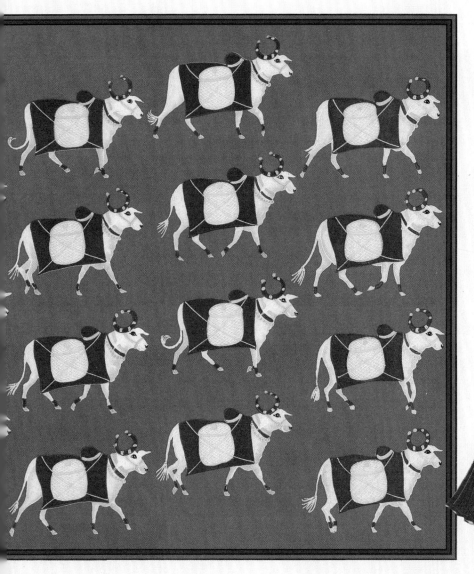

On the twenty-seventh day, thirty-two Brahma bulls were needed to deliver sixty-four baskets of rice.

The raja was deeply troubled. "One grain of rice has grown very great indeed," he thought. "But I shall fulfill the reward to the end, as a raja should."

On the twenty-ninth day, Rani was presented with the contents of two royal storehouses.

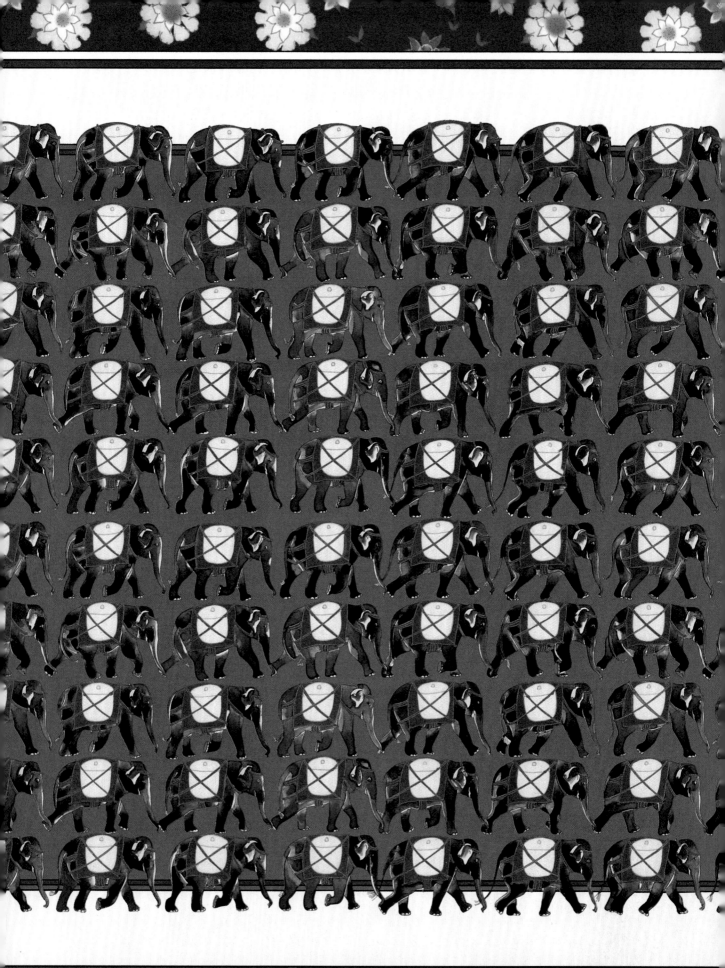

On the thirtieth and final day, two hundred and fifty-six elephants crossed the province, carrying the contents of the last four royal storehouses—five hundred and thirty-six million, eight hundred and seventy thousand, nine hundred and twelve grains of rice.

All together, Rani had received more than one billion grains of rice. The raja had no more rice to give. "And what will you do with this rice," said the raja with a sigh, "now that I have none?"

"I shall give it to all the hungry people," said Rani. "And I shall leave a basket of rice for you, too, if you promise from now on to take only as much rice as you need."

"I promise," said the raja.

And for the rest of his days, the raja was truly wise and fair, as a raja should be.

About the Author/Illustrator

Demi

Demi Hitz prefers to be known by her first name only. Demi has been around artists all of her life. Her mother was an artist and her father was an architect and actor. When she was younger, Demi lived in India for two years. Her love of Indian art shows up in *The Hallowed Horse: A Folktale from India* and *One Grain of Rice.*

Demi loves to travel. Her travels have influenced her to write books about different people and places around the world. She has written about the explorer Marco Polo and his travels through Asia. She also has written books about China: *Dragon Kites and Dragonflies, A Chinese Zoo,* and *Chen Ping and His Magic Axe.*

Several of Demi's books have won awards, including *The Empty Pot* and *The Nightingale.*

In addition to writing and illustrating books, Demi gives speeches at colleges and libraries about her work.

Reader Response

Open for Discussion

When would Rani be a good person to have with you? Explain.

Comprehension Check

1. Both *Ananse's Feast* and *One Grain of Rice* take place during a famine in which some characters feast while others go hungry. Look back at both stories and make two lists to show which characters feast and which characters go hungry.

2. Would the raja have given Rani as much rice if she had asked for it all at once? What in the story supports your answer?

3. What kind of person is Rani? Use examples from the story to support your ideas.

4. Compare and contrast the lives of the raja and the rice farmers. Where do they live? Who is in charge? (Compare and Contrast)

5. Contrast the raja's plan for the rice at the beginning of the story with what the raja really did with the rice. (Compare and Contrast)

 Test Prep

Look Back and Write

Look back through the story. What kind of person is the raja at the beginning of the story? How does he change by the end? Use details from the story to explain your answer.

One of the Greatest Inventions

by Philip Carona

Numerals we use look like this:

0	1	2	3	4
5	6	7	8	9

Where did they come from? Long before the Romans were using letters to express number ideas, people in India were writing numerals. They looked like this.

Indian numerals

= 1
= 2
= 3
= 4
= 5
= 6
= 7
= 8
= 9

113

The people were called Hindus, and they had nine number signs. With nine number signs the Hindus could write any numeral.

These numerals were easy to read. They were easy to work with.

If a man wanted to buy three sheep, he wrote it this way:

If he wanted to buy thirty-three sheep, he wrote it this way:

Each three had a "place value"— three ones and three tens.

If he wanted to buy three hundred thirty-three sheep, he wrote it this way:

Each three had a place—three ones, three tens, and three hundreds.

He had a number pattern. It was based on ten.

How could he write three hundred and three? There were no tens. He left a space and wrote it this way:

This sometimes led to trouble. If a man wrote ३ ३ he might get only thirty-three because his numeral was hard to read.

As time went on, the Hindus began using a dot to show there was no number in that place. They wrote ३•३ and this was better. This means three hundreds, no tens, and three ones.

Later this small dot became a circle. The circle is now called ZERO.

The Hindus had created one of the world's greatest inventions. It was the numeral zero.

Zero is the number sign that means "no quantity—nothing."

Predicting

- To **predict** means to tell what you think might happen next in a story, judging from what has already happened.

- A prediction is what you think will happen.

- As you read, use the clues in the story and what you know from real life to help you decide what might happen next.

Read "What to Do with an Old Hat," from *Uncle Nacho's Hat* **by Harriet Rohmer.**

Talk About It

1. What clues from the story and from your own life helped you make your prediction?

2. How close was your prediction to what really happened?

What to Do with an Old Hat

by Harriet Rohmer

Uncle Nacho put on the new hat and looked at himself in the mirror.

"See how handsome it makes you look, Uncle Nacho," said Ambrosia.

"It's true. All the girls will fall in love with me."

"That's for sure, Uncle Nacho. Well, I have to go to school now. I'll come by later."

"Take care of yourself, Ambrosia. And thank you for the hat."

"Now I have a new hat," said Uncle Nacho to himself. "But what am I going to do with this old hat that's not good for anything anymore?"

"Hat," he said to his old hat. "What am I going to do with you?"

"I know. I'll put you in my trunk."

"Wait a minute. What if mice get in and start to eat you? No, no, no. I'd better not put you in my trunk."

> **Predict what Uncle Nacho will do with his old hat.**

"But hat, you're really not good for anything anymore," said Uncle Nacho. "You don't keep me dry in the rain. I should throw you away. I'll just take you outside right now and throw you away in the street."

"Wait a minute. I think I see a car coming. You might get run over. No, no, no. I'd better not throw you away in the street."

"But hat, you're really not good for anything anymore," said Uncle Nacho. "You don't keep the sun off my head. I should throw you away. I'll just take you outside right now and throw you in the trash."

"There! May some good man find you. Someone who will appreciate you. A decent person."

LOOK AHEAD

In *The Woman Who Outshone the Sun,* Lucia must decide whether or not to return the town's river. Read and see if you can predict what she will do.

117

Vocabulary

Words to Know

cruel	spied	arrived
shone	thirst	respect
astonished	excitement	

Words with opposite meanings are **antonyms.** You can figure out the meaning of an unknown word by looking for a clue in nearby words. Sometimes this clue is an antonym.

Read the paragraph below. Notice how *left* helps you understand its antonym *arrived*.

Heroes in the Neighborhood

Cruel winds whipped the trees and shook houses. In the excitement of the storm, I was astonished to see my tree house fly through the air! Finally, the storm left almost as quickly as it had arrived. I spied rescue workers coming up the street. I respect them, because they help people. I even gave one water to ease his thirst. The sun soon shone and made the damage look even worse.

Write About It

Write a headline about a hero you know. Use some vocabulary words.

THE WOMAN WHO OUTSHONE THE SUN

THE LEGEND OF LUCIA ZENTENO

from a poem by Alejandro Cruz Martinez • pictures by Fernando Olivera
retold by Harriet Rohmer and David Schecter

The day Lucia Zenteno arrived, everyone in the village was astonished. No one knew where she came from. Yet they all saw that she was amazingly beautiful, and that she brought thousands of dancing butterflies and brightly-colored flowers on her skirts. She walked softly yet with quiet dignity, her long, unbraided hair flowing behind her. A loyal iguana walked at her side.

No one knew who she was, but they did know that nothing shone as brightly as Lucia Zenteno. Some people said that Lucia Zenteno outshone the sun. Others said that her glorious hair seemed to block out the light.

Everyone felt a little afraid of someone so wonderful and yet so strange.

There used to be a river that ran by the town, almost the same river that runs by there now. And people said that when Lucia Zenteno went there to bathe, the river fell in love with her. The water rose from its bed and began to flow through her shining black hair.

When Lucia finished bathing, she would sit by the river and comb out her hair with a comb made from the wood of the mesquite tree. And when she did, the water, the fishes, and the otters would flow out of her hair and return to the river once more.

The old people of the village said that although Lucia was different from them, she should be honored and treated with respect. She understood the ways of nature, they said.

But some people did not listen to the elders. They were afraid of Lucia's powers, which they did not understand. And so they refused to answer Lucia's greetings, or offer their friendship. They called her cruel names and spied on her day and night.

Lucia did not return the meanness of the people.
She kept to herself and continued to walk with her
head held high.

Her quiet dignity angered some of the people. They
whispered that Lucia must be trying to harm them. People
became more afraid of Lucia and so they treated her
more cruelly. Finally, they drove her from the village.

Lucia went down to the river one last time to say good-bye. As always, the water rose to greet her and began to flow through her glorious hair. But this time when she tried to comb the river out of her hair, the river would not leave her.

And so, when Lucia Zenteno left the village, the river and the fishes and the otters went with her, leaving only a dry, winding riverbed, a serpent of sand where the water had been.

Everyone saw that Lucia Zenteno was leaving and that the river, the fishes, and the otters were leaving with her. The people were filled with despair. They had never imagined that their beautiful river would ever leave them, no matter what they did.

Where once there had been green trees and cool breezes, now no more rain fell, no birds sang, no otters played. The people and their animals suffered from thirst. People began to understand, as never before, how much the river, the fishes, the otters, even the trees and birds had meant to the village. They began to understand how much the river had loved Lucia Zenteno.

The elders said that everyone must search for Lucia
and beg her forgiveness. Some people did not want to.
They were too afraid. But when the drought continued,
everyone finally agreed to follow the elders' advice. And
so the whole village set out in search of Lucia.

After many days of walking, the people found the iguana cave where Lucia had gone to seek refuge. Lucia was waiting for them, but they could not see her face. She had turned her back to the people.

At first no one dared say a word. Then two children called out, "Lucia, we have come to ask your forgiveness. Please have mercy on us and return our river!"

Lucia Zenteno turned and looked at the people. She saw their frightened, tired faces, and she felt compassion for them. At last she spoke. "I will ask the river to return to you," she said. "But just as the river gives water to all who are thirsty, no matter who they are, so you must learn to treat everyone with kindness, even those who seem different from you."

The people remembered how they had treated Lucia, and they hung their heads in shame.

Seeing that the people were truly sorry for what they had done, Lucia returned with them to the village and began to comb out her hair. She combed out the water, she combed out the fishes, she combed out the otters, and she kept on combing until the river had returned once more to where it belonged.

The people were overjoyed to have their river again. They poured water over themselves and over their animals, they jumped into the river, and they laughed and cried with happiness.

In all the excitement, no one noticed at first that Lucia had disappeared again. When the children asked the elders where she had gone, the elders replied that Lucia had not really left them. Though they would not be able to see her, she would always be there, guiding and protecting them, helping them to live with love and understanding in their hearts.

About the Authors

ALEJANDRO CRUZ MARTINEZ, HARRIET ROHMER, DAVID SCHECTER

Alejandro Cruz Martinez was a Zapotec Indian poet who lived in Oaxaca, Mexico. Because he wanted the history of his people to live on, Mr. Martinez collected stories and wrote them down as poems. One of these poems is about the legendary character Lucia Zenteno. After Mr. Martinez died, his widow sent the poem to a children's book publisher. The publisher showed the poem to Harriet Rohmer and David Schecter, who turned it into a story.

About the Illustrator

FERNANDO OLIVERA

Fernando Olivera is an artist who was a good friend of Alejandro Cruz Martinez. When Mr. Martinez told him the story, Mr. Olivera was so interested that he painted pictures of what he thought Lucia Zenteno looked like. After Mr. Martinez died and the book about Lucia was written, Mr. Olivera created the pictures to go with it. Mr. Olivera lives in the state of Oaxaca, Mexico.

Reader Response

Open for Discussion
Would you like to live in the village after Lucia Zenteno took the river away with her? Why or why not?

Comprehension Check

1. Remember that in folk tales, fables, or legends the characters often either teach a lesson or learn a lesson. Now, why do you think Lucia came to the village? Use details from the story to support your answer.

2. Look back at the story. Why was the river important to the people of the village?

3. How will the villagers treat the next stranger who comes to their village? Use story details to support your answer.

4. What did you **predict** would happen when Lucia left the village the first time? Were you right? (Predicting)

5. Did you **predict** what Lucia would do when the villagers went to the iguana cave to see her? What did you base your prediction on? (Predicting)

Test Prep
Look Back and Write
Look back on page 131. Use details to explain what happened when Lucia tried to comb the river out of her hair and why it happened.

135

Iguana

by Trevor Smith

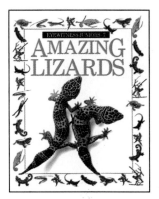

IN SOUTH AND CENTRAL AMERICA, iguanas are the biggest and most common lizards. They are found from deserts to rain forests, and there are more than 120 different kinds in the West Indies alone.

NASTY TAIL
This Mexican iguana has a long, spiked tail that it lashes at its enemies.

DIVING FOR SEAWEED
The marine iguana is the only lizard in the world that feeds under the sea. After a good meal of seaweed, it suns itself on rocks.

ANY FRIES WITH THAT?
Central American Indians have always liked iguana meat. You can even buy iguana burgers in snack bars in Panama.

GUMS OF STEEL
The Galapagos Islands are the home of huge land iguanas. These strange lizards spend their days nibbling nothing but cactus.

OUT OF THE EGG
The mother iguana lays her eggs under a log or in a hole in the ground. Then she leaves them. When the baby iguanas hatch, they have to look after themselves.

RHINOCEROS IGUANAS
These huge lizards have little horns on their foreheads. They may look fierce, but most of them eat nothing but plants.

FLASHY COLORS
Many male iguanas are more colorful than the females. They use their flashy outfits to attract the females.

The flaps of skin that hang off an iguana's throat are called its dewlap.

Going Through the Old Photos

by Michael Rosen

Who's that?
That's your Auntie
    Mabel
and that's me
under the table.

Who's that?
That's Uncle Billy.
Who's that?
Me being silly.

Who's that
licking a lolly?
I'm not sure
but I think it's Polly.

Who's that
behind the
    tree?
I don't know,
I can't see.
Could be you.
Could be me.

Who's that?
Baby Joe.
Who's that?
I don't know.

Who's that
    standing
on his head?
Turn it round.
It's Uncle Ted.

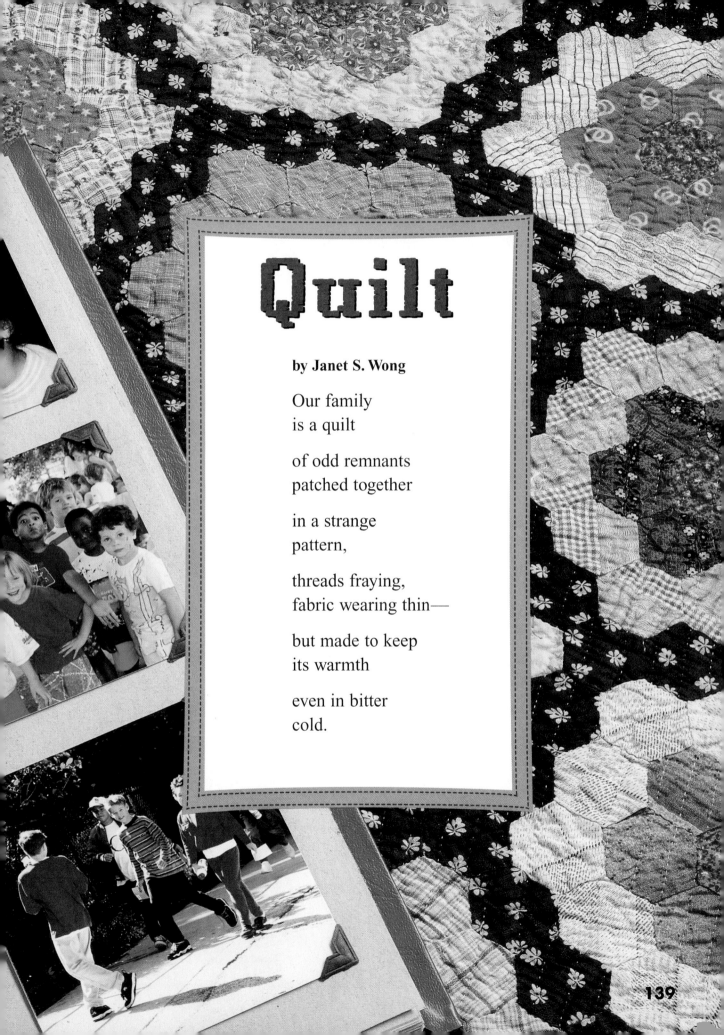

Quilt

by Janet S. Wong

Our family
is a quilt

of odd remnants
patched together

in a strange
pattern,

threads fraying,
fabric wearing thin—

but made to keep
its warmth

even in bitter
cold.

The Stars

by Nelly Palacio Jaramillo

Always quiet,
Always blinking,
By day sleeping,
At night winking.

Las estrellas

por Nelly Palacio Jaramillo

Siempre quietas,
Siempre inquietas,
Durmiendo de día,
De noche despiertas.

Sky Bear

by the Mohawk Indians

Long ago,
three hunters and their little dog
found the tracks of a giant bear.
They followed those tracks
all through the day
and even though it was almost dark
they did not stop, but continued on.
They saw that bear now, climbing
    up
a hill, which glittered
with new-fallen snow.
They ran hard to catch it,
but the bear was too fast.
They ran and they ran, climbing
up and up until one of the hunters
    said,
"Brothers, look down."
They did and saw they
were high above Earth.
That bear was Sky Bear,
running on through the stars.
Look up now
and you will see her,
circling the sky.

WRAP-UP

How can our traditions and the traditions of others make our lives more interesting?

COME FOR DINNER

Write a Cookbook

Ananse's Feast, Thunder Cake, and *One Grain of Rice* are all stories about sharing food. Choose foods from the stories and traditional foods from your family. Share them in a cookbook titled *Foods We Like to Share.*

1. **Select** three or four foods.

2. **Find** a recipe for each food.

3. **Write** a cookbook. Include pages that have a recipe and a drawing of each food. Design a title page.

A LiTTLe LuCKY MoNeY

Write About a Good Choice

Sam has four dollars of lucky money to spend in *Sam and the Lucky Money.* Each member of your group has four lucky dollars. How will your group spend all of the money?

1. **Skim** the story to recall the choices Sam has for spending his money. Then brainstorm other choices.

2. **Write** about the best choice. Why is it the best choice?

ANiMAL SAFARi

Report on Animals

In *The Woman Who Outshone the Sun,* Lucia has an iguana that follows her around. Work with a group to report on animals from this unit.

1. **List** the animals in the unit and choose three to research.

2. **Report** on each animal's usual habitat. Locate on a map or globe where each one can be found.

PUPPeT TALK

Perform a Puppet Show

What was your favorite story in Unit 4? Retell it with classmates, using stick puppets.

1. **Choose** a story. Decide who will be the puppeteer for each character.

2. **Make** stick puppets for the characters and practice the story from beginning to end.

3. **Perform** your puppet show for others.

Test Talk

Answer the Question

Use Information from the Text

Some test questions tell you to support your answer with details from the text. To answer such questions correctly, you must include information from the text.

A test about "The Fox and the Stork," pages 34–37, might have this question.

Test Question 1

What is Fox's biggest problem? Use details from the fable to support your answer.

Understand the question.

Read the question carefully to find the key words. Finish the statement "I need to find out . . ."

Decide where you will look for the answer.

The answer may be *right there* in one place, or you may have to *think and search* for it. The answer may depend on the *author and you.* Make notes about details that answer the question.

Check your notes.

Reread the question and your notes. Ask yourself, "Do I have enough information?" If details are missing, go back to the selection.

See how one student uses information from the text to answer the question.

I think Fox's biggest problem is that he can't eat the soup. On page 37 the Narrator says that Fox's soup was served in a long-necked jar with a narrow top. I'll note that and finish reading.

I'm right! Fox's biggest problem is that he can't eat the soup that Stork serves, and he is hungry. I'll look back at the question to see if I have the right information.

Try it!

Now use what you have learned to answer these test questions about "The Fox and the Stork," pages 34–37.

Test Question 2

Compare how Stork feels before dinner at Fox's house and after. Use details from the fable to support your answer.

Test Question 3

How are Fox and Stork alike and different? Use details from the story to support your answer.

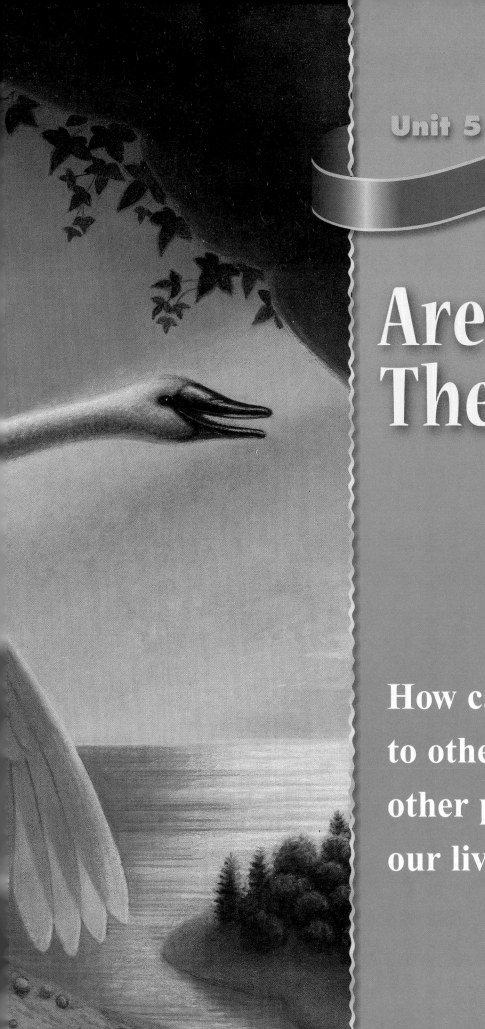

Are We There Yet?

How can visits to other times and other places make our lives better?

Making Judgments

- A judgment is your opinion about a character, a situation, an action, or an idea in a story or article.

- When you **make judgments,** you use what you already know and what you have read.

- Find sentences from the story or article to support your judgments.

Read "Grandpa's Memories" from *Grandpa Is a Flyer* by Sanna Anderson Baker.

Talk About It

1. Is the boy being fair when he says he will weed the garden if his dad takes him to see the plane? Why or why not?

2. Does Dad do the right thing in taking the boy to see the plane? Explain.

Grandpa's Memories
by Sanna Anderson Baker

Once I'd seen a plane in the sky I couldn't think about anything else. Every day my brother, Erik, and I rushed through our chores. We had to milk our cow, gather eggs, haul water, and bring in wood so we could get inside to hear "The Air Adventures of Jimmy Allen."

One day the noise of a plane nearly raised our roof. I banged out the screen door and squinted to see. It was so low and so loud, I knew the plane had to be landing. I begged Dad to take me.

Finally, when I promised to weed the garden, he said, "Get in!" We rattled up one dusty road and

down another in the Model A until we saw the plane sitting in Conrad Johnson's field.

The pilot was dressed like Lindbergh in a flying suit and boots, but he had his goggles off, so I could see it wasn't Lindy. He was a barnstormer, a pilot who'd land in a farmer's field and sell rides.

"Ready for a ride, young man?" he asked me. I just shook my head. I didn't have any money, and I knew my dad didn't, either. But it didn't cost anything to look, and I looked over every inch of that Jenny.

After awhile our neighbor R.V. Carlson handed over his money and climbed into the cockpit. Seeing that plane take off was like watching a miracle.

That night I told Erik, "By next summer I'm going to fly."

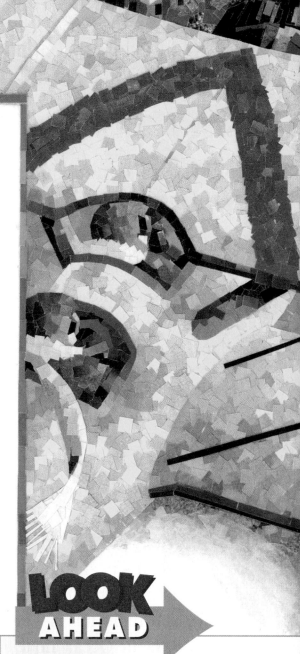

In *Flight: The Journey of Charles Lindbergh,* Charles Lindbergh makes the first solo flight across the Atlantic Ocean from New York to Paris. Read and judge for yourself if he makes good decisions.

Vocabulary

Words to Know

compasses	engine	flight
instruments	route	soars

Words that are pronounced the same but have different spellings and meanings are called **homophones.** To understand the meaning of a homophone look for clues around the word.

Read the paragraph below. Why is the word *soars* used and not *sores?*

Flight Journal

I check my flight <u>instruments</u>. My <u>compasses</u> show I head straight east, so I am on the correct <u>route</u>. If my <u>engine</u> doesn't run into trouble, I should be in Paris in eight hours. As my plane <u>soars</u> through the sky, I think about the landing ahead. What a <u>flight</u> this is—my first time across the Atlantic Ocean alone!

Write About It

Imagine you're landing the plane. Write a journal entry using vocabulary words.

FLIGHT

The Journey of Charles Lindbergh

by Robert Burleigh • illustrated by Mike Wimmer

It is 1927, and his name is Charles Lindbergh.
Later they will call him the Lone Eagle. Later they
will call him Lucky Lindy. But not now. Now it is
May 20, 1927, and he is standing in the still-dark
dawn. He watches rain drizzle down on the airfield.
And on his small airplane. The airplane has a
name painted on its side: *Spirit of St. Louis*.

Lindbergh is nearly as tall as the plane itself. And yet—he is about to attempt what no one has done before: to fly—without a stop—from New York to Paris, France. Over 3,600 miles away. Across the Atlantic Ocean. Alone.

He climbs into the boxlike cockpit that will be his only home for many, many hours. He clicks on the engine. He listens as it catches, gurgles, and roars. A few friends are here to say good-bye. They are only a few feet away, and yet to Lindbergh how far off they seem. They look up at him and wave. "Good luck! Keep safe!"

A telephone wire stretches across the far end of the field. To touch this wire will plunge the plane to the ground. There is an extra fuel tank in front of the cockpit. Because of this, Lindbergh cannot see straight ahead. Will the *Spirit of St. Louis*, with its over 5,000 pounds, rise into the air? To keep the plane lighter, Lindbergh is leaving behind his radio and parachute. Will that be enough?

He has been up all night getting ready. A thought runs back and forth through his mind: It is still possible to turn back. To return home. And yet another thought is stronger: I have been waiting my entire life for this flight. Lindbergh lowers his goggles and nods his head: "Go!"

Men on each side push to help the plane roll over the soggy ground. The little plane bumps forward, gaining speed. The wheels leave the ground, then touch back. The plane seems to hop, taking its "last bow to earth." On the third try it stays aloft. It soars above the wire by only twenty feet. The

Spirit of St. Louis rises in the air. It is 7:52 in the morning, New York time. Lindbergh points his plane toward the Atlantic and beyond, toward Paris. Over thirty hours away.

He gazes down in the morning light. How far off Paris seems—across the long ocean. He plans to follow the coastline, flying northeast. The land's edge looks to him like green fingers, pointing at the dark sea. To see ahead, Lindbergh pokes a small homemade periscope out the side of the cockpit. Sometimes he flies very close to the water. Just ten feet above the waves. He knows that at this low height the plane glides more smoothly. The plane drones on. It cruises at about 100 miles an hour. At this rate, he will have enough fuel to reach his destination, but only if he stays on course.

Beside him in the cockpit is a little book. He keeps a diary as he goes all day long, hour by hour. It is as if he were speaking to himself. He wants to remember everything. Because no one else will ever really know. At 12:08 he flies above Nova Scotia. Just after 4:00 he flies above the coast of Newfoundland. At dusk he looks down and sees icebergs! In his diary he calls them "White pyramids . . . White patches on a blackened sea; sentries of the Arctic." He wonders what lies ahead.

The sun sets far behind the plane. Lindbergh flies over St. John's, Newfoundland, the last point of land in North America. Now he can no longer follow the land's edge for direction. He must chart his course carefully. The slightest movement could send him miles off course and risk the fuel supply. He follows two compasses and the stars to navigate. As long as the sky is clear, he is safe. But he must stay awake. He writes: "Now I must cross not one, but two oceans: One of night and one of water."

Time passes slowly. It is almost 9:00 at night, Lindbergh's thirteenth hour in the air. He has completed one-third of the flight. He moves through dense, curling fog, lit ghostly white by the moon. He suddenly enters a huge stormcloud. The plane shimmers, moving up and down in the uniform blackness. He wonders: Can I fly above it? Slowly, he soars to 10,500 feet. Here it is clear—but very, very cold. He extends his arm outside the cockpit and feels "stinging pinpricks."

He clicks on his small flashlight and peers out: Heavy ice has formed on the plane's wings. He cannot risk his instruments' icing up. He points the *Spirit of St. Louis* back down. The wings quiver as they slice through the turbulent air. The fog continues but now, at least, the air is warmer. The ice begins to melt and Lindbergh roars ahead, through the fog and clouds, to Paris over 2,000 miles away.

Space and time and deep, deep darkness: It is the other side of midnight, the loneliest hours. Lindbergh has been awake for almost fifty hours straight. He is closer to Europe than America. Now there is no turning back, only moving forward. He dozes for a minute and then jerks awake. One of the plane's wings is dipping crazily.

In a sudden rush of fear, he grabs for the throttle. He gropes for the steady center with his heart pounding. As he feels the leveling wings, he lets out breath. He repeats over and over to himself: *I must not sleep, I must not sleep*. Here, high above the churning ocean, to sleep is to die!

These are some of the things he does to stay awake: He leans his face near the open window to feel the cold air. He holds his eyelids up with his fingers to keep them from closing. He remembers growing up on a farm in Minnesota. He remembers being a trick pilot, and walking out on a plane's wings. He remembers the people in St. Louis who

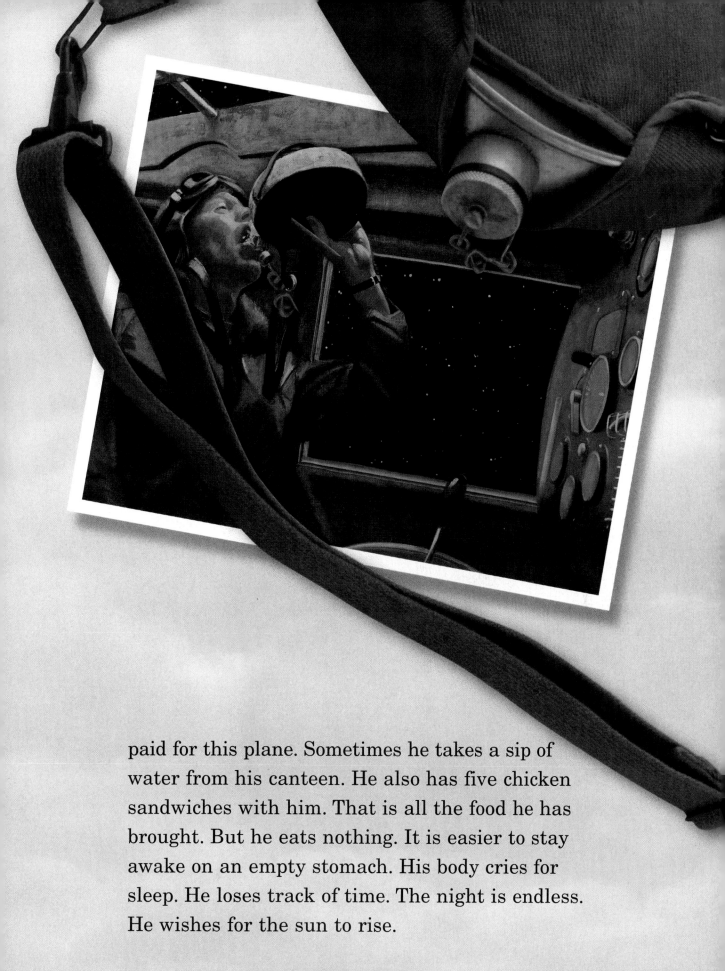

paid for this plane. Sometimes he takes a sip of
water from his canteen. He also has five chicken
sandwiches with him. That is all the food he has
brought. But he eats nothing. It is easier to stay
awake on an empty stomach. His body cries for
sleep. He loses track of time. The night is endless.
He wishes for the sun to rise.

Dawn comes slowly, growing out of the gray mist. "Will the fog never end?" he wonders. The clouds change color: "from green to gray, and from gray to red and gold." Lindbergh has been in the air for twenty-three hours. He is 2,300 miles from New York and has 1,300 miles to go. He feels completely alone in the world. He feels as if he were "flying through all eternity." He tries to stay on course. But because of his constantly curving route, he is not always sure. Here and there, the clouds seem to break apart. He sees, far below him, the ocean. From high up it is like a great blue shaft, with gray walls. Then he flies into the clouds again. Into the unchanging mist.

The day comes on, brighter and warmer. Sometimes he imagines he sees land. No: it is only the flickering shapes of the clouds. And water, water, water, endless water. It is 7:30 in the morning in New York, and Paris is over a thousand miles away. "There's no alternative but death and failure," he writes. Flying closer to the water, Lindbergh sights a porpoise, leaping above the waves. He spies a seagull. Then fishing boats. Something quickens in Lindbergh's blood. He guides the *Spirit of St. Louis* carefully down and down, to just above a boat. He throttles the plane and calls out a question: "Which way," he shouts, "is Ireland?" He hopes for a word. He longs for a wave, ". . . a warmer welcome back to the fellowship of men." It is 10:52 in the morning, New York time.

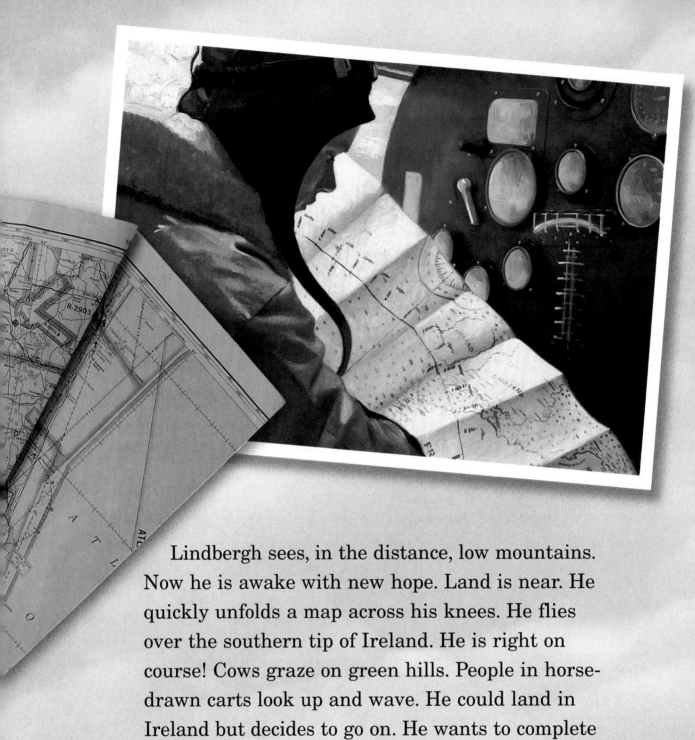

Lindbergh sees, in the distance, low mountains. Now he is awake with new hope. Land is near. He quickly unfolds a map across his knees. He flies over the southern tip of Ireland. He is right on course! Cows graze on green hills. People in horse-drawn carts look up and wave. He could land in Ireland but decides to go on. He wants to complete his dream.

It is 1:52 in the afternoon, New York time, as he crosses England. It is Lindbergh's thirty-first hour in the air. He crosses more water. The wide day is slowly ebbing toward twilight. When he sees land—the coast of France—children run out of their houses and watch him fly by. He continues on.

Then Lindbergh spies a glow ahead of him. Paris! *I am here, I am here.* A great joy wells up inside him. For a moment, he does not want the flight ever to end. Huddled inside his tiny box-house, folded in the dense hum of the airplane's engine, he loves this strange closeness to the clouds and sky. It is 4:52 in the afternoon, New York time. Lindbergh's thirty-fourth hour in the air.

From above, all Lindbergh sees are many, many small lights. But now he must concentrate on just one thing: "the sod coming up to meet me."

Closer, closer, closer: The plane touches the ground. It bounces, rolls, hugs the solid earth. It is 10:22, Paris time. The flight has taken thirty-three and a half hours.

Thousands of people are running toward the plane. For a moment, Lindbergh is dazed. It seems to him as if he were "drowning in a great sea." People surround the plane, cheering. But Lindbergh can hardly hear them. His ears seem to have been deafened by the hours of roaring engine.

Crowds pull him out of the cockpit. Men and women are calling his name, over and over.

They carry him on their shoulders. Others begin to tear pieces of the plane. More than anything else, Lindbergh wants to save the *Spirit of St. Louis*. His first words are a question: "Are there any mechanics here?" But no one speaks English. Finally, two French aviators arrive to help him. Policemen guard the plane. The aviators take Lindbergh away from the still-cheering crowd.

In the airfield's hangar, he tells the story of his flight to the other pilots: The cramped cockpit, the aloneness, the long, long night. Meanwhile, unknown to Lindbergh, newspaper headlines all over the world are beginning to blazon the news: AMERICAN HERO SAFE IN PARIS! Lindbergh is driven off to the American Embassy. He answers more questions about his flight. He has not slept in over sixty hours. Finally, at 4:15 in the morning he goes to bed.

When he wakes, his life will be changed forever. When he wakes, there will be huge parades and medals and speeches. He will be the most famous man in the world.

It is the year 1927. It is 1927, and his name is Charles Lindbergh.

About the Author
Robert Burleigh

As a child, Robert Burleigh mostly liked sports. "I do remember writing a little rhymed poem (about a cowboy) as a very young child, which I still have," he recalls. When he grew up, Mr. Burleigh got a job at a publishing company. A big part of his job there was writing scripts for videos and filmstrips. This helped him to become a better writer.

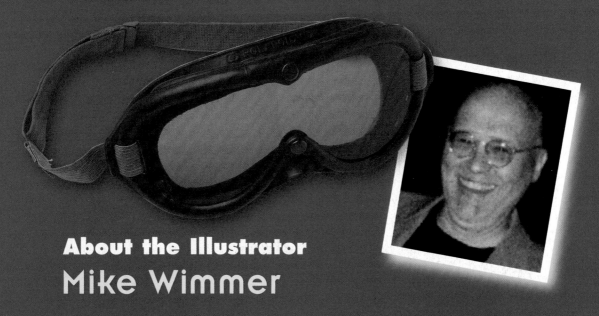

About the Illustrator
Mike Wimmer

As an artist, Mike Wimmer started young. "Comic book heroes and sports figures were my main subjects." He also read classic adventure stories like *Robinson Crusoe*. "I didn't know what an illustrator was," Mr. Wimmer remembers, "but I did know that someone painted these pictures and that I wanted to be that person." Now he has become a well-respected illustrator himself.

Reader Response

Open for Discussion

Pretend you are an invisible passenger with Lindbergh. What do you see, hear, feel?

Comprehension Check

1. Today's airplanes have very high-tech equipment for navigation, but Lindbergh had very little help finding his way. Look back through the selection. List the things Lindbergh used to navigate from New York to Paris.

2. Was Lindbergh afraid during his flight? Point out parts of the text that support your answer.

3. Look back at pages 158–159. Why would the people of St. Louis have been especially interested in Lindbergh's flight?

4. Lindbergh used many tricks for staying awake. **Make a judgment** about whether they were good tricks. Support your response with facts from the story. (Making Judgments)

5. Everyone was excited about Lindbergh's flight. **Make a judgment** about why people today aren't as interested when someone flies across the Atlantic. Support your answer with facts. (Making Judgments)

🦉 Test Prep
Look Back and Write

Look back through the story. What was the author's purpose for writing about Charles Lindbergh? Did he want to express or describe something, to inform, to entertain, or to persuade you? Use details from the story to support your answer.

A Place in the Sky

by Ron Fridell

Test Prep

How to Read a Biography

1. Preview

- A biography is the written story of someone's life—in chronological order.

- Scan the text and look for the important dates in Bessie Coleman's life.

2. Read and Make a Time Line

- Read the biography to find out the order of events in Bessie Coleman's life. Use a time line to help you remember them.

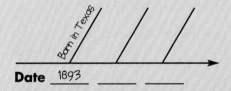

Date 1893 ____ ____

3. Think and Connect

Think about *Flight: The Journey of Charles Lindbergh.* Then look over your time line from "A Place in the Sky."

How are Bessie Coleman and Charles Lindbergh alike? How are they different?

During her first air shows, Bessie tried out different outfits. Many of them looked like military uniforms.

★ ★ ★ ★ ★ ★ ★ ★ ★ ★ ★ ★ ★ ★ ★

Have you ever dreamed that you could fly a plane? Bessie Coleman had that dream, and she made that dream come true, but it wasn't easy.

169

Bessie's first airplane was a Curtiss JN-4, or Jenny. It was made mainly of wires, wood, and canvas. Even with careful maintenance the engine often stalled in flight.

★ ★

Bessie Coleman was born in Atlanta, Texas, in 1893. During World War I (1914–1918), she read all about the daring pilots who fought each other in the sky over Europe. *I belong up there too,* she decided.

But no flying school in America would take Bessie Coleman. In the early 1900s, flying was still new—and dangerous. Planes had open cockpits, and crashes were so common that pilots were known as "flying fools." Women pilots were rare, and an African American woman pilot? Never. There was no place in the sky

for Bessie Coleman, not in America.

Then Bessie read about Americans who'd gone to France to find their place in the sky. Jacques Bullard, an African American pilot, flew with the French in the war. Harriet Quimby, the first American woman flyer, went to France to get her pilot's license. If they could do it, so could Bessie Coleman.

She made the trip across the Atlantic by ocean liner, landing in France in November of 1920. Not long after that, she began taking flying lessons. On June 15, 1921, Bessie Coleman earned her

★ ★

Photographs like this were likely to be printed in African American-owned newspapers in areas where Bessie made her flights.

★ ★

pilot's license. She'd found her place in the sky.

When Bessie returned to the U.S., she brought a new dream back with her. She wanted to open her own flying school and teach other African American women and men to fly. To make this dream come true, she flew around the country putting on air shows. During one of these shows, in Orlando, Florida, in 1926, a wrench slid into the control gears, and her plane went into a dive. Bessie was thrown from the cockpit—this was before pilots wore seatbelts— and hurled to her death.

Nearly five thousand people attended Bessie Coleman's funeral. They came to honor the first African American woman to pilot a plane. In the years to come many other African American women and men would find their own place in the sky, thanks in part to Bessie Coleman.

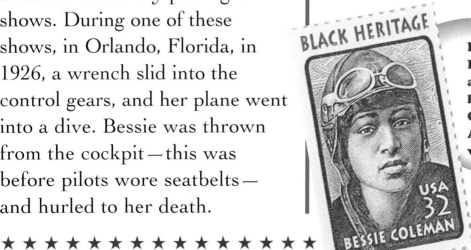

In 1995 the U.S. Postal Service issued a 32-cent stamp in honor of Bessie Coleman, the first African American woman pilot.

★ ★

Skill Lesson

Fact and Opinion

- A **statement of fact** can be proved true or false.

- A **statement of opinion** is what someone believes or thinks and cannot be proved true or false.

- Words that express what someone feels or thinks, such as *believe, could, like,* and *good,* are clues to a statement of opinion.

Read "Moving Along on Bike Trails" by Stewart Warren from *The Herald News.*

Write About It

1. Find a statement of opinion that tells what *could* be done. Write it down.

2. Find a statement of fact that tells why a bike trail would be a good idea. Write it down.

Moving Along on Bike Trails

by Stewart Warren, Staff Writer

PLAINFIELD—As Kathy Felix and Michelle Bigger drove Monday to the meeting on the park district's bike path plan, they realized pedaling would be faster.

The two neighbors, residents of the Indian Oaks subdivision, got stuck in traffic while trying to get to the Plainfield Township Park District's administration offices, 100 W. Ottawa St.

"If there had been a clear way across Illinois 59, we could have been here in 10 minutes," Bigger said.

Like many other people in the village, Felix and Bigger want more places to ride their bicycles.

"We take our kids out biking all the time," Felix said. "Some of the

172

back roads are so busy, we can't take them without fear."

To meet the need, park district officials want to create a township-wide bike trail system to serve everyone—people who ride for recreation, and those who use bikes as transportation.

"Our district has done community-wide surveys in the past," said Greg Bott, park district director. "The recreational opportunity with the highest demand was bicycling. And we are trying to respond to that."

Although the routes haven't been planned yet, one trail could be built along the DuPage River. If it were built, the path could connect Plainfield with Naperville, Joliet, and Bolingbrook, said John Vann, assistant director for parks and planning.

LOOK AHEAD

Chibi
A True Story from Japan

by Barbara Brenner and Julia Takaya
illustrated by June Otani

In *Chibi: A True Story from Japan,* a mother duck decides to raise her babies in a busy downtown park. Read and notice statements of fact and opinion about the choices the mother duck makes.

Vocabulary

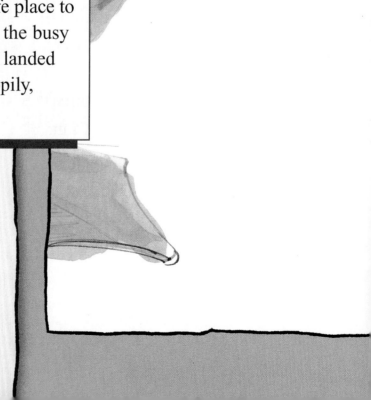

Words to Know

| avenue | pool | splash |
| ducklings | nest | spring |

When you read, you may come across a word you don't know. To figure out its meaning, look for clues near it. A definition or an example given near the unknown word may be a clue.

Notice how *ducklings* is used in the paragraph. Look for a definition near it to find what it means.

No Place Like Home

Just like every spring, animals were getting ready to have babies. Mother Duck looked for a place to build a nest where she could raise her ducklings. The baby ducks needed a safe place to live. Mother Duck marched straight up the busy avenue, avoiding the cars. Splash! She landed in a pool in the park. She splashed happily, knowing she had found a home.

Write About It

Draw the duck family. Write a caption. Use some vocabulary words.

Chibi

A True Story from Japan

by Barbara Brenner and Julia Takaya
illustrated by June Otani

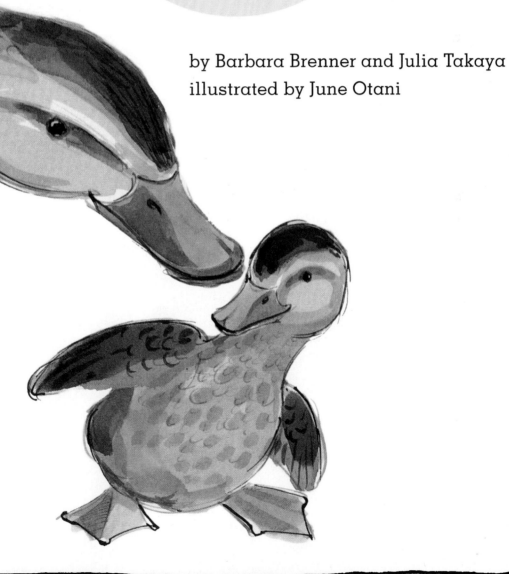

One spring morning a brown-and-gold duck flew over a skyscraper in Tokyo, Japan.

Far below her she spied a pool of water gleaming like glass. She dipped down and glided onto it, hardly making a splash. After a quick look around, the duck settled down in a clump of ivy by the pool and proceeded to build her nest.

It didn't seem to bother her that she was in an office park in downtown Tokyo . . . or that she was only a stone's throw away from Uchibori *Dori*, the eight-lane avenue where three hundred cars a minute roar in and out of the city. The duck went right on with her work.

Soon the nest held ten ivory-colored eggs. The *oka-san* brooded them herself, turning the eggs gently with her feet from time to time so they would keep warm on all sides.

Twenty-six days later there was a commotion in the ivy. One egg cracked, and a wet little baby duck pecked its way out of the shell. Then another egg hatched, then seven more. Within hours there were nine fluffy ducklings in the ivy, snuggled under their mother's warm brood feathers.

It seemed as if the tenth egg might be a dud. But on the next day it finally cracked open and a very small and scraggly duckling pushed out of the shell. Oka-san patiently moved the other ducklings about in the nest to make room for this last and tiniest member of the family.

As soon as number ten was fluffed out and steady on her feet, the mother duck led her entire brood out of the nest and onto the ledge above the pool.

That was when the workers in the offices
in Mitsui Office Park saw the ducks for the first
time. The ducks caused a sensation. Word spread
like wildfire. *Eleven wild* kamo *are living around
the pool!*

People began to visit the park just to watch the
duck family and to take pictures of them. Among
the duck watchers was a news photographer,
Mr. Sato, who gave a name to the tiniest duckling.
Sato-san named her *Chibi*, which means "tiny."

Every day the crowd grew larger. People
brought lunch in their kerchiefs to eat beside
the pool so they could watch Oka-san and her
ducklings. Vendors moved in with hot-noodle
carts, carts of *oden* (steamed vegetables) and
isobe maki (rice cakes wrapped in seaweed)
and with ice-cream and cake carts.

Tokyo TV started to broadcast a "Duck Watch"
on the evening news. School children came on
class trips to see the *kamo* family. Photographers
came to take pictures. Sato-san was there
every day.

Soon four thousand people a day were visiting the Mitsui Office Park to see Oka-san and her ducklings. Chibi was clearly their favorite. Everyone worried about her. Being the smallest and youngest, she struggled to catch up with her brothers and sisters, who had already learned Waddle, Line Up, Follow the Leader, and Belly-whopper Splash. When Chibi finally learned to dive under the water to get moss to eat, everyone celebrated. "Chibi! Chibi!" they chanted. Sato-san took the first pictures of Chibi "bottoms up."

One morning in June, Oka-san hastily quack-quacked the ducklings together. When they were all in a line, she marched them to one of the exits and right out of the office park! Sato-san and the other duck watchers trailed after her at a safe distance. When she reached the corner, Oka-san stopped short, turned, and waddled all the way back to the pool, her ducklings right behind her.

She repeated the trip seven times that morning.

"What is that crazy Oka-san doing?" people asked one another. Sato-san thought he knew. The duck family had outgrown the little pool at the office park. But right across the street was an ideal place for growing ducklings—the great moat in the Emperor's Gardens. Oka-san was going to take her family there. She was planning to cross Uchibori *Dori!*

But when? Nobody knew, not even Sato-san. The police were notified to be on the alert. They would stop traffic for the ducks. Sato-san and some of the other photographers brought sleeping bags and prepared to spend the night. Many of them had traveled a long way to capture on film the exciting moment when the *kamo* crossed the eight-lane avenue.

Night came, and lights went on in the city. The moon came out. Everything was quiet around the little pond. As dawn broke, the duck watchers listened for the first sounds of activity in the ivy. But the duck family slept on.

At eleven o'clock in the morning, Oka-san was still asleep, her head tucked under her wing. Chibi and the other ducklings were paddling around in the pool, chasing water spiders. Could it be that Mama Duck had changed her mind? Sato-san took out his shaver and freshened up a bit. He passed around a thermos of *ocha*. But the hot green tea couldn't take away the effects of a sleepless night. Some of the photographers decided to leave. Others dozed in their camp chairs and sleeping bags. To pass the time, Sato-san took pictures of his friends sleeping.

At exactly noon, the mother duck lifted her bill, stood up, and waggled her tail. Was the bill or the tail the signal? The ducklings gathered behind their mother—Chibi first, then the others. Marching single file, they followed Oka-san to the exit. But—wait! She wasn't leading them to where the watchers had gathered. Oka-san was heading for the *opposite* exit.

Sato-san was the first to realize what she meant to do. Frantically he dialed the police. Then, camera in hand, he clambered over the azalea bushes and raced along the divider to the other exit.

The street crossing light was changing from *midori* to *akai*—green to red. Oka-san ignored it. Looking straight ahead, she waddled down from the curb. Chibi and the other ducklings did the same. At that moment a sports car came speeding down the broad avenue. It was heading straight for the ducks. Sato-san, who was about to take a picture, dropped his camera and ran into the street. Waving his arms frantically, he shouted at the driver to stop. *"Tomatte! Tomatte!"*

The car swerved. Brakes screeched. Police whistles blew. Flashbulbs went off. But Oka-san paid no attention. Calmly she herded her brood across four lanes, up onto the divider, then down onto the remaining four lanes.

Within minutes the *kamo* family had crossed the wide avenue and had reached the other side safely.

Mama Duck flew down into the moat first. She paddled around, encouraging her family to join her. One by one they obeyed, tumbling over the steep rocky sides and plopping into the green water.

Only Chibi was left teetering on the edge of the high wall. She quacked mournfully. Her brothers and sisters were already swimming away from her with Oka-san, who seemed not to realize that Chibi had been left behind.

Sato-san called to the duckling. "Go on, Chibi, you can make it."

Now Oka-san turned back and swam toward Chibi, quacking anxiously. Chibi looked down at the water. It was far, far down. The top of the wall must have seemed as high as Mount Fuji to her. She gave one final quack and—

Splash! Chibi joined her family in the garden moat of the Emperor of Japan.

That night the front page of every Tokyo newspaper featured the duck story. Sato-san was disappointed that he hadn't gotten a picture of the *kamo* crossing Uchibori *Dori*. But he was happy that he was the one who had helped the duck family to cross the avenue safely.

Japanese word	Say it this way	It means
akai	*ah kah ee*	red
Chibi	*Chee bee*	tiny
dori	*doh ree*	street or avenue
isobe maki	*ee soh beh mah kee*	rice cakes usually wrapped in seaweed
kamo	*kah moh*	duck or ducks
midori	*mee doh ree*	green
ocha	*oh cha*	green tea
oden	*oh den*	steamed fish and vegetables
Oka-san	*Oh kah sahn*	Mother
Sato-san	*Sah toh sahn*	Sato is a last name; San means respected (Mrs., Mr., or Miss)
tomatte	*toh mah teh*	stop

About the Authors
Barbara Brenner and Julia Takaya

When Barbara Brenner had her first baby, Mark, she wanted to write children's books. "I thought to myself, 'So few words! Such simple ideas! I can write one of these during Mark's nap time.' Was I ever wrong!"

When Julia Takaya watched a mother duck raising her ducklings in the middle of Tokyo, she thought others would be as interested as she was in the duck family, so she and Barbara Brenner wrote about Chibi.

Reader Response

Open for Discussion

Why did so many people come to watch Chibi and the rest of the duck family?

Comprehension Check

1. Think about the setting. How would the selection be different if the duck had laid her eggs in the country rather than in a city? Use details from the story to help you answer.

2. Look back on page 190. Do you think traffic on a city street should be stopped to let animals cross? Why or why not?

3. Is Oka-san a good mother or a foolish one? How can you tell? Support your answer with details from the story.

4. Which sentence states a **fact** and which states an **opinion?**
   - Chibi was the cutest duckling in her family.
   - Chibi was the smallest duckling in her family.

   (Fact and Opinion)

5. Write a **fact** that you learned about Chibi. Write a statement of **opinion** about Chibi.

   (Fact and Opinion)

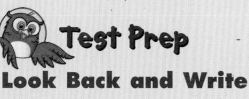 Test Prep

Look Back and Write

Look back on pages 180–181. How do the people show they care about the duck family? Why do you think they care? Use the text and pictures to support your answer.

The Physical World

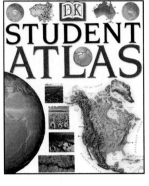

THIS MAP SHOWS the main physical features of the world: the mountain ranges, the great rivers and lakes, deserts, grassland plains, seas, and oceans. Try to find Japan on the map. Notice that Japan is a string of islands in the Pacific Ocean.

NORTHERN HEMISPHERE

THE WORLD: FACTS AND FIGURES

- LOWEST POINT ON LAND: Dead Sea, West Asia 1,312 ft. below sea level
- HIGHEST POINT: Mount Everest, China/Nepal 29,035 ft.
- LOWEST POINT (OCEAN): Mariana Trench, Pacific Ocean 36,201 ft. below sea level
- LONGEST RIVER: Nile, Africa 4,132 miles
- LARGEST OCEAN: Pacific Ocean 63,800,000 sq. miles
- LARGEST LAKE: Caspian Sea, Asia 142,200 sq. miles

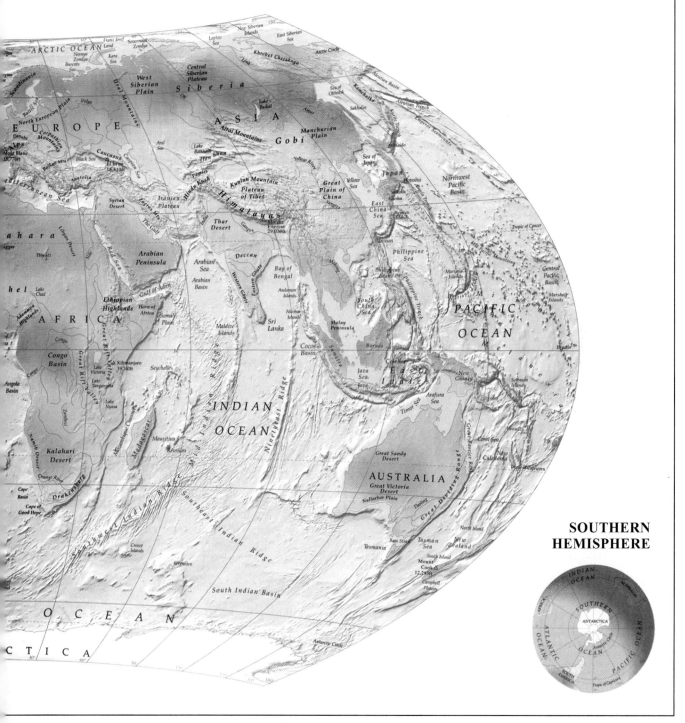

SOUTHERN HEMISPHERE

Predicting

- To **predict** means to tell what you think might happen next in a story based on what has already happened.

- A prediction is what you say will happen.

- As you read, use what you know from your own life and from what you've learned and look for clues in the story that help you decide what might happen next.

Read "Keep the Buckets Coming" from *A Little Excitement* by Marc Harshman.

Talk About It

1. What clues from the story and from your own life helped you make your prediction?

2. How close was your prediction to what really happened?

Keep the Buckets Coming

by Marc Harshman

A fire, set in the woodburning stove, has gotten out of hand.

. . . Side by side with Annie I worked, quietly and hard and quickly, to keep the buckets coming to Dad. Later I saw his hands bloody from fighting to keep a hold on that slippery roof. *Roar* and *whoosh* were the sounds the fire made, and I was more scared than excited. . . .

Eventually the Piney Volunteer Fire Department gathered: Jimmy up from Adeline, and Harry from Dutch Fork, Bob from Clouston, and Dan Creary from Sleepy Creek Hollow. They all came in pickups since the pump truck was frozen up solid over at Dixon's. Neighbors from across the valley and down the ridge would arrive, too, before it was over. But, of course, the first one there was Dad himself—he joked later that no one had ever been quicker than that to a fire, and if they had, he'd eat his Sunday pants.

> **Predict what will happen now that the volunteer fire department has arrived.**

The night was beautiful, all white and black beyond the fire. Somewhere in that black a deer must have lifted her nose from grass pawed clear of snow, looked over our way, and wondered—too smart and too quick to be scared. I felt better when I heard Jimmy and Bob, Harry and Dan shouting and laughing, even when it seemed they shouldn't. But finally we watched the orange flames fall back until one hour after it had started, Bob Jackson shone his flashlight down the flue and announced: "She's all gone, folks! Get on in the house and get to bed." And of course, we didn't. . . .

LOOK AHEAD

In *Brave Irene*, Irene faces dangers as she tries to deliver the dress to the duchess on time. Will she be able to do it, or will the storm stop her? Read and predict what will happen.

Vocabulary

Words to Know

howling	whipped	wind
snatched	whirled	stumble

Words that are spelled the same but pronounced differently are called **homographs.** Homographs also have different meanings. To know which meaning is correct look for clues in nearby sentences.

Read the paragraph. Decide if *wind* rhymes with *find* and means "go in a crooked way" or rhymes with *skinned* and means "air in motion."

Saving Sam

The <u>wind</u> was blowing stronger and faster. The wind's <u>howling</u> made a terrible noise. The flag <u>whipped</u> on the pole outside. Vic knew he had to find his dog Sam. Vic could barely walk in the wind—he could only <u>stumble</u>. Suddenly, he heard a bark. He <u>whirled</u> around to find Sam behind him. Vic quickly <u>snatched</u> Sam up and took him inside.

Talk About It

Use vocabulary words to discuss a storm you've seen or been in.

Brave Irene

written and illustrated by William Steig

Mrs. Bobbin, the dressmaker, was tired and had a bad headache, but she still managed to sew the last stitches in the gown she was making.

"It's the most beautiful dress in the whole world!" said her daughter, Irene. "The duchess will love it."

"It *is* nice," her mother admitted. "But, dumpling, it's for tonight's ball, and I don't have the strength to bring it. I feel sick."

"Poor Mama," said Irene. "I can get it there!"

"No, cupcake, I can't let you," said Mrs. Bobbin. "Such a huge package, and it's such a long way to the palace. Besides, it's starting to snow."

"But I *love* snow," Irene insisted. She coaxed her mother into bed, covered her with two quilts, and added a blanket for her feet. Then she fixed her some tea with lemon and honey and put more wood in the stove.

With great care, Irene took the splendid gown down from the dummy and packed it in a big box with plenty of tissue paper.

"Dress warmly, pudding," her mother called in a weak voice, "and don't forget to button up. It's cold out there, and windy."

Irene put on her fleece-lined boots, her red hat and muffler, her heavy coat, and her mittens. She kissed her mother's hot forehead six times, then once again, made sure she was tucked in snugly, and slipped out with the big box, shutting the door firmly behind her.

It really was cold outside, very cold. The wind whirled the falling snowflakes about, this way, that way, and into Irene's squinting face. She set out on the uphill path to Farmer Bennett's sheep pasture.

By the time she got there, the snow was up to her ankles and the wind was worse. It hurried her along and made her stumble. Irene resented this; the box was problem enough. "Easy does it!" she cautioned the wind, leaning back hard against it.

By the middle of the pasture, the flakes were falling thicker. Now the wind drove Irene along so rudely she had to hop, skip, and go helter-skeltering over the knobby ground. Cold snow sifted into her boots and chilled her feet. She pushed out her lip and hurried on. This was an important errand.

When she reached Apple Road, the wind decided to put on a show. It ripped branches from trees and flung them about, swept up and scattered the fallen snow, got in front of Irene to keep her from moving ahead. Irene turned around and pressed on backwards.

"Go home!" the wind squalled. "Irene . . . go hooooooome . . ."

"I will do no such thing," she snapped. "No such thing, you wicked wind!"

"Go ho—o—ome," the wind yodeled. "GO HO—WO—WOME," it shrieked, "or else." For a short second, Irene wondered if she shouldn't heed the wind's warning. But no! *The gown had to get to the duchess!*

The wind wrestled her for the package—walloped it, twisted it, shook it, snatched at it. But Irene wouldn't yield. "It's my mother's work!" she screamed.

Then—oh, woe!—the box was wrenched from her mittened grasp and sent bumbling along in the snow. Irene went after it.

She pounced and took hold, but the ill-tempered wind ripped the box open. The ball gown flounced out and went waltzing through the powdered air with tissue-paper attendants.

Irene clung to the empty box and watched the beautiful gown disappear.

How could anything so terribly wrong be allowed to happen? Tears froze on her lashes. Her dear mother's hard work, all those days of measuring, cutting, pinning, stitching . . . for *this?* And the poor duchess! Irene decided she would have to trudge on with just the box and explain everything in person.

She went shuffling through the snow. Would her mother understand, she wondered, that it was the wind's fault, not hers? Would the duchess be angry? The wind was howling like a wild animal.

Suddenly Irene stepped in a hole and fell over with a twisted ankle. She blamed it on the wind. "Keep quiet!" she scolded. "You've done enough damage already. You've spoiled everything! *Everything!"* The wind swallowed up her words.

She sat in the snow in great pain, afraid she wouldn't be able to go on. But she managed to get to her feet and start moving. It hurt. Home, where she longed to be, where she and her mother could be warm together, was far behind. It's got to be closer to the palace, she thought. But where any place was in all this snow, she couldn't be sure.

She plowed on, dragging furrows with her sore foot. The short winter day was almost done.

Am I still going the right way, she wondered. There was no one around to advise her. Whoever else there was in this snow-covered world was far, far away, and safe indoors—even the animals in their burrows. She went plodding on.

Soon night took over. She knew in the dark that the muffled snow was still falling—she could feel it. She was cold and alone in the middle of nowhere. Irene was lost.

She had to keep moving. She was hoping she'd
come to a house, any house at all, and be taken in.
She badly needed to be in someone's arms. The snow
was above her knees now. She shoved her way
through it, clutching the empty box.

She was asking how long a small person could
keep this struggle up, when she realized it was
getting lighter. There was a soft glow coming from
somewhere below her.

She waded toward this glow, and soon was
gazing down a long slope at a brightly lit mansion.
It had to be the palace!

Irene pushed forward with all her strength and—*sloosh! thwump!*—she plunged downward and was buried. She had fallen off a little cliff. Only her hat and the box in her hands stuck out above the snow.

Even if she could call for help, no one would hear her. Her body shook. Her teeth chattered. Why not freeze to death, she thought, and let all these troubles end. Why not? She was already buried.

And never see her mother's face again? Her good mother who smelled like fresh-baked bread? In an explosion of fury, she flung her body about to free herself and was finally able to climb up on her knees and look around.

How to get down to that glittering palace? As soon as she raised the question, she had the answer.

She laid the box down and climbed aboard. But it pressed into the snow and stuck. She tried again, and this time, instead of climbing on, she leaped. The box shot forward, like a sled.

The wind raced after Irene but couldn't keep up. In a moment she would be with people again, inside where it was warm. The sled slowed and jerked to a stop on paving stones.

The time had come to break the bad news to the duchess. With the empty box clasped to her chest, Irene strode nervously toward the palace.

But then her feet stopped moving and her mouth fell open. She stared. Maybe this was impossible, yet there it was, a little way off and over to the right, hugging the trunk of a tree—the beautiful ball gown! The wind was holding it there.

"Mama!" Irene shouted. "Mama, I found it!"

She managed somehow, despite the wind's meddling, to get the gown off the tree and back in its box. And in another moment she was at the door of the palace. She knocked twice with the big brass knocker. The door opened and she burst in.

She was welcomed by cheering servants and a delirious duchess. They couldn't believe she had come over the mountain in such a storm, all by herself. She had to tell the whole story, every detail. And she did.

Then she asked to be taken right back to her sick mother. But it was out of the question, they said; the road that ran around the mountain wouldn't be cleared till morning.

"Don't fret, child," said the duchess. "Your mother is surely sleeping now. We'll get you there first thing tomorrow."

Irene was given a good dinner as she sat by the fire, the moisture steaming off her clothes. The duchess, meanwhile, got into her freshly ironed gown before the guests began arriving in their sleighs.

What a wonderful ball it was! The duchess in her new gown was like a bright star in the sky. Irene in her ordinary dress was radiant. She was swept up into dances by handsome aristocrats, who kept her feet off the floor to spare her ankle. Her mother would enjoy hearing all about it.

Early the next morning, when snow had long since ceased falling, Mrs. Bobbin woke from a good night's sleep feeling much improved. She hurried about and got a fire going in the cold stove. Then she went to look in on Irene.

But Irene's bed was empty! She ran to the window and gazed at the white landscape. No one out there. Snow powder fell from the branch of a tree.

"Where is my child?" Mrs. Bobbin cried. She whipped on her coat to go out and find her.

When she pulled the door open, a wall of drift faced her. But peering over it, she could see a horse-drawn sleigh hastening up the path. And seated on the sleigh, between two large footmen, was Irene herself, asleep but smiling.

Would you like to hear the rest?

Well, there was a bearded doctor in the back of the sleigh. And the duchess had sent Irene's mother a ginger cake with white icing, some oranges and a pineapple, and spice candy of many flavors, along with a note saying how much she cherished her gown, and what a brave and loving person Irene was.

Which, of course, Mrs. Bobbin knew. Better than the duchess.

About the Author/Illustrator
William Steig

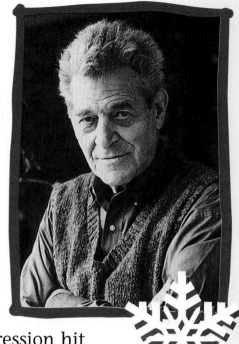

William Steig has created many wonderful stories. How does he start? "First of all I decide it's time to write a story," he says. "Then I say, 'What shall I draw this time? A pig or a mouse?' Or, 'I did a pig last time; I'll make it a mouse this time.' Then I start drawing."

When Mr. Steig was young, the Depression hit his family hard, and they lost all of their money. Since Mr. Steig's brothers were either married or too young to earn a living, it was up to him to help the family. "The only thing I could do was draw," he says. "Within a year I was selling cartoons to the *New Yorker* [magazine] and supporting a family." He drew cartoons for many years before a co-worker suggested he try creating a children's book.

Mr. Steig finds illustrating a book a lot harder than just drawing pictures. He says, "I love to draw, and I love to write—but I hate to illustrate. When you draw, you draw anything that wants to come out, but when you illustrate you have to draw someone who has on a polka-dot dress. It has to be the same as the previous picture. You have to remember what it says in the story."

Reader Response

Open for Discussion

If you were playing a game, would you like to have Irene on your team? Why or why not?

Comprehension Check

1. Tell two events in the story that show how much Irene cares about her mother.

2. Why is it important to Irene to get the gown to the duchess? Is that a good enough reason for Irene to take the risks she takes? Support your answer with details from the story.

3. Both Irene and Charles Lindbergh are brave. What other qualities do they share? Use details to support your answer.

4. As you were reading, what did you **predict** would happen when Irene first went out into the blizzard? On what did you base your prediction? (Predicting)

5. As you were reading, what did you **predict** would happen when Irene got to the palace? On what did you base your prediction? (Predicting)

Test Prep
Look Back and Write

Look back at pages 208–212. Why did Irene choose to go on to the palace after the wind snatched the dress from the box? Use details from the text to support your answer.

Water on Earth

How to Read a Textbook Lesson

1. Preview

- Textbooks are school books. Textbook lessons contain facts about a topic and often include questions or activities at the end. What is the topic of this lesson?

2. Read and Use Questions

- Read the questions at the end of the lesson first. Then answer the questions as you read the lesson.

How do rain and snow form?

3. Think and Connect

Think about *Brave Irene*. Then look over your answers to the questions in "Water on Earth."

The water cycle has three steps. Which step took place when Irene was bringing the dress? Which step took place the next morning?

WHEN IS IT GOING TO RAIN?

from Grade 3, Scott Foresman
Discover the Wonder Science Program

Notice the clouds in the picture below. If you saw these clouds, would you want to get out your umbrella and boots? You might. Dark clouds often bring rain.

RAINING AND SLEETING

Water vapor rises into the cool air high above the Earth. Then the water vapor condenses on invisible bits of dust and salt in the air, forming droplets. Clouds are made of billions of these tiny droplets.

CLOUDS OFTEN GET DARK BEFORE A STORM.

How Big Is a Raindrop?

In the tropics, near the equator, the air is very warm. So most clouds in the tropics are made of tiny water droplets, but not bits of ice. A drop of water in a cloud is very tiny, but not as small as a speck of dust.

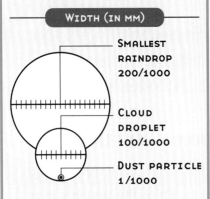

WIDTH (IN MM)

SMALLEST RAINDROP 200/1000

CLOUD DROPLET 100/1000

DUST PARTICLE 1/1000

Rain will only fall if the cloud droplets join and become at least as large as the small raindrop shown above. The average raindrop is much bigger and is made of many cloud droplets.

What Did You Find Out?
1. How wide is a cloud droplet?
2. Do you think you could see one cloud droplet? Why?
3. How many times wider is the small raindrop than the cloud droplet?

What happens to water droplets high in the air where temperatures are below freezing? If you said that water droplets freeze into bits of ice, you're right.

Water droplets keep freezing onto the ice bits, making them larger and larger. The bits of ice become too heavy to float in the air. Then these bits of ice fall down through the clouds. They fall to the ground as snowflakes.

Water in any form that falls from clouds is called **precipitation** (pri sip′ ə tā′ shən). Snow is one kind of precipitation that you may have seen.

Suppose the air temperatures near the ground are above freezing. Would snowflakes fall? You probably figured out that warm air makes ice melt. That's right. In warmer temperatures, the bits of ice that fall from the clouds melt into raindrops. Rain is another kind of precipitation.

Suppose raindrops pass through a thick layer of very cold air close to the earth. These raindrops freeze before they can fall. This kind of precipitation is called sleet. You can even hear sleet rattle when it hits the ground!

WHAT MIGHT HAPPEN TO THIS PUDDLE? IT MIGHT EVAPORATE.

THE WATER CYCLE

The rainstorm finally is over. You see puddles of water everywhere. You might even feel like splashing in a puddle like the child on page 222 is doing. The sky looks clear now. Suddenly, the sun begins shining brightly. Later, you notice that the puddles have disappeared.

What happened to the water in the puddles? Light energy from the sun causes the water to evaporate. The water vapor can condense into water droplets, forming clouds. These water droplets can freeze. What happens when bits of ice in clouds become too heavy to stay in the air? You already learned the answer to that question. Precipitation falls from the clouds.

The process of evaporation, condensation, and precipitation is called the **water cycle.** Trace the three steps of the water cycle shown in the picture. The entire water cycle keeps repeating itself over and over again.

CHECKPOINT

1. How do rain and snow form?

2. What are the steps in the water cycle?

3. **Take action!** Place a small mirror into a freezer for a few minutes. Remove the mirror and breathe on it. What forms on the mirror? Explain why.

THE WATER CYCLE

CONDENSATION
PRECIPITATION
EVAPORATION

INTO THE FIELD

What do clouds look like?

Go outside and observe clouds once a day for two weeks. Record what you see. Describe how the clouds are alike and different.

Author's Purpose

- The **author's purpose** is the author's reason for writing.

- An author may try to express or to describe something in a way that gives the reader a feeling about or sets the mood of the scene.

- Another purpose is that an author may try to entertain the reader.

Read "Tomás Visits the Library" from *Tomás and the Library Lady* by Pat Mora.

Talk About It

1. What mood or feeling did you get as you read about Tomás?

2. How does the author give you this feeling?

Tomás
Visits the Library
by Pat Mora

Tomás stood in front of the library doors. He pressed his nose against the glass and peeked in. The library was huge!

A hand tapped his shoulder. Tomás jumped. A tall lady looked down at him. "It's a hot day," she said. "Come inside and have a drink of water. What's your name?" she asked.

"Tomás," he said.

"Come, Tomás," she said.

Inside it was cool. Tomás had never seen so many books. The lady watched him. "Come," she said again, leading him to a drinking fountain. "First some water. Then I will bring

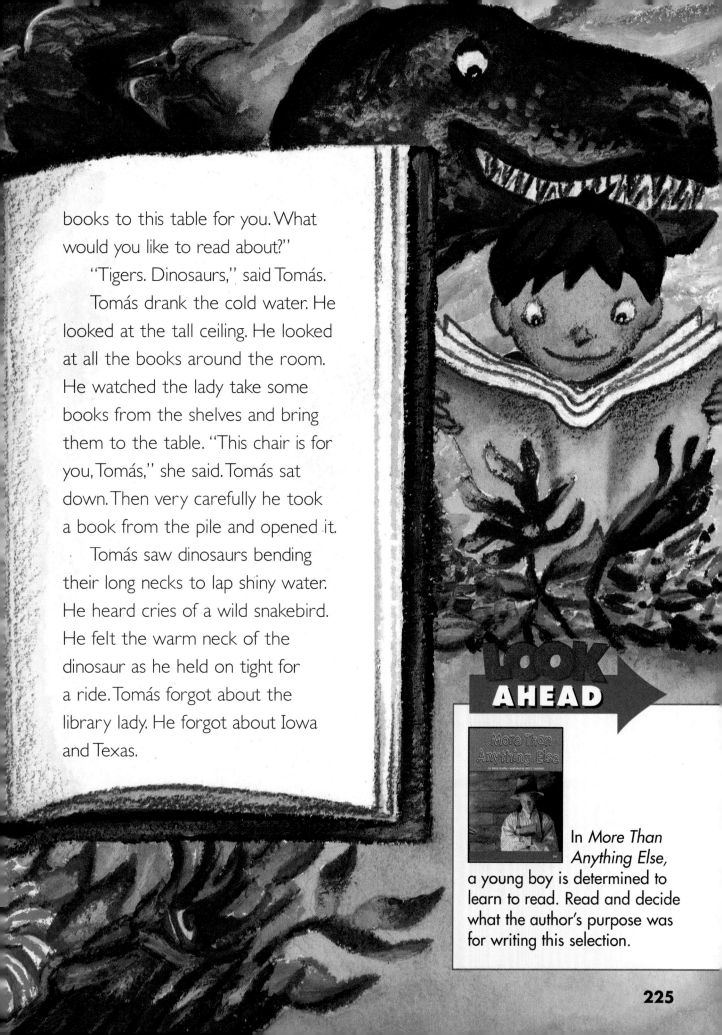

books to this table for you. What would you like to read about?"

"Tigers. Dinosaurs," said Tomás.

Tomás drank the cold water. He looked at the tall ceiling. He looked at all the books around the room. He watched the lady take some books from the shelves and bring them to the table. "This chair is for you, Tomás," she said. Tomás sat down. Then very carefully he took a book from the pile and opened it.

Tomás saw dinosaurs bending their long necks to lap shiny water. He heard cries of a wild snakebird. He felt the warm neck of the dinosaur as he held on tight for a ride. Tomás forgot about the library lady. He forgot about Iowa and Texas.

LOOK AHEAD

In *More Than Anything Else,* a young boy is determined to learn to read. Read and decide what the author's purpose was for writing this selection.

Vocabulary

Words to Know

alphabet	magic	cabin
newspaper	learning	tales

Words that are pronounced the same but spelled differently, such as *tales* and *tails,* are called **homophones.** Homophones also have different meanings. To understand the difference between them, look for clues in nearby sentences.

Read the paragraph. Why is the word *tales* used below and not *tails?*

A Good Lesson to Learn

I grew up in a <u>cabin</u>. To get the job I wanted, I needed to read. So I started by <u>learning</u> the letters of the <u>alphabet</u>. Then, almost as if by <u>magic</u>, I could read whole words! I could even read articles in a <u>newspaper</u>. I learned to read and write so well that I have written some best-selling <u>tales</u>!

Write About It

What has been hard for you to learn? Write a journal entry about it. Use some vocabulary words.

More Than Anything Else

by Marie Bradby / illustrated by Chris K. Soentpiet

Before light—while the stars still twinkle—Papa,
my brother John, and I leave our cabin and take
the main road out of town, headed to work.

The road hugs the ridge between the Kanawha
River and the mountain. We travel it by lantern.
My stomach rumbles, for we had no morning meal.
But it isn't really a meal I want, though I would
not turn one down.

More than anything else, I want to learn to read.

But for now, I must work. From sunup to sundown, we pack salt in barrels at the saltworks.

A white mountain of salt rises above Papa's head. All day long we shovel it, but it refuses to grow smaller.

We stop only to grab a bite—sweet potatoes and corn cakes that Papa has brought along in his coat pocket. As I eat every crumb of my meal, I stare at the white mountain. Salt is heavy and rough. The shiny white crystals leave cuts on your hands, your arms, your legs, the soles of your feet.

My arms ache from lifting the shovel, but I do not think about the pain there. I think about the hunger still in my head—reading. I have seen some people—young and old—do it. I am nine years old and I know, if I had a chance, I could do it too.

I think there is a secret in those books.

In the chill of the evening, I follow Papa and John back up the road, stopping to catch a frog. The frog wiggles and slips, but I hold on tight and let go when I want to.

There is something different about this place where we live now. All people are free to go where they want and do what they can. Book learning swims freely around in my head and I hold it long as I want.

Back in town, coal miners, river men, loggers, and coopers gather on the corner. They are worn-out as me, but full of tales.

I see a man reading a newspaper aloud and all doubt falls away. I have found hope, and it is as brown as me.

I see myself the man. And as I watch his eyes move across the paper, it is as if *I* know what the black marks mean, as if *I* am reading. As if everyone is listening to *me*. And I hold that thought in my hands.

I will work until I am the best reader in the county. Children will crowd around me, and I will teach *them* to read.

But Papa taps me on the shoulder. "Come on." And John tugs at my shirt. They don't see what I see. They don't see what I can be.

We hurry home. "Mama, I have to learn to read,"
I say. She holds my hand and feels my
hunger racing fast as my heart.

It is a small book—a blue the color of midnight. She gives it to me one evening in the corner of our cabin, pulling it from under the clothes that she washes and irons to make a little money.

She doesn't say where she got it. She can't read it herself. But she knows this is something called the alphabet. She thinks it is a sing-y kind of thing. A song on paper.

After work, even though my shoulders still ache and my legs are stained with salt, I study my book. I stare at the marks and try to imagine their song.

I draw the marks on the dirt floor and try to figure out what sounds they make, what story their picture tells.

But sometimes I feel I am trying to jump without legs. And my thoughts get slippery, and I can't keep up with what I want to be, and how good I will feel when I learn this magic, and how people will look up to me.

I can't catch the tune of what I see. I get a salt-shoveling pain and feel my dreams are slipping away.

I have got to find him—that newspaper man.
I look everywhere.
Finally, I find that brown face of hope.

He tells me the song—the sounds the marks make.
I jump up and down singing it. I shout and
laugh like when I was baptized in the creek.
I have jumped into another world and I am saved.

But I have to know more. "Tell me more," I say.

"What's your name?" he asks.

"Booker," I say.

And he takes the sound of my name and draws
it on the ground.

I linger over that picture. I know I can hold it
forever.

Marie Bradby

More Than Anything Else is Marie Bradby's first children's book. She has also worked as a newspaper reporter and written articles for *National Geographic* magazine. She lives in Louisville, Kentucky, with her family.

About the Illustrator

Chris K. Soentpiet

Chris K. Soentpiet came to the United States from Korea when he was eight years old. Before he created the pictures for the book *More Than Anything Else,* he visited the Booker T. Washington National Monument in Hardy, Virginia. He studied the life of Booker T. Washington. When he made the pictures of young Booker and his family, Mr. Soentpiet wanted to make sure the pictures were true to life.

Reader Response

Open for Discussion

What would you say to nine-year-old Booker if you could join him in one of the pictures? How might you help him?

Comprehension Check

1. Why didn't Booker learn to read in school as many children today do? Use details from the story to support your answer.

2. How do you think the newspaper man learned to read?

3. From the story, you can tell that Booker's family is poor. Find details in the story that support this conclusion.

4. The **author's purpose** is the writer's reason for writing. Give one important purpose the author might have had for writing about Booker. Why do you think this? (Author's Purpose)

5. Often an **author** has more than one **purpose** for writing. Give another reason the author might have had for writing about Booker. Why do you think so? (Author's Purpose)

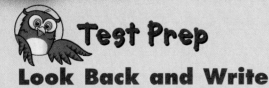 Test Prep

Look Back and Write

Look back on pages 236–237. Explain why Booker says his thoughts get slippery as he looks at the book his mother gave to him.

Like Booker, in More Than Anything Else, *Mary McLeod Bethune believed in the importance of education.*

$1.50 and a Dream

by Toni A. Watson

Mary McLeod Bethune was a dreamer. Great achievers usually are. But she knew that without hard work, a dream can quickly fade.

In 1898, after years of schooling and teaching, Mary McLeod married Albertus Bethune, a former teacher. A year later, Albert McLeod Bethune was born. But Bethune's teaching days were not over. She had a dream: to start a school for African American girls. In the summer of 1904, Bethune packed a few clothes and, with her young son, caught a train to Daytona Beach, Florida.

When Bethune stepped off that train in Daytona Beach, she had $1.50 in her purse and a dream in her heart. During her search for a suitable site for her school, she located a two-story frame building on Palm Street. The owner asked for $11 a month rent. She said she had only $1.50 for a down payment but promised the rest by the end of the month. The owner agreed. When the neighborhood people heard that she intended to start a school, they came to help. The women brought mops and brooms; the men had saws, hammers, and nails.

Bethune begged boxes and packing crates from nearby stores. At the city dump, she found a barrel for her desk and charcoal for the girls to write with. She discovered discarded dishes, pans, and lamps behind some Daytona Beach hotels.

Bethune and her students in 1905

On October 3, 1904, the Daytona Normal and Industrial Institute for Negro Girls opened with five girls and Albert Bethune as pupils. Bethune decided that her students would learn both lessons from books and how to earn a living. She said they would be trained "in head, hand, and heart."

By 1923, the school was doing well, but steady financial support was necessary. One hundred miles away, Jacksonville's Cookman Institute, an all-male training school for African Americans, had stopped growing. Later that year, the two schools merged to become the Bethune-Cookman Collegiate Institute. Bethune was the institute's first president. In 1941, the school became a four-year liberal arts college.

Bethune lived on and off at Bethune-Cookman College until her death on May 18, 1955. The marker on her grave there reads "Mother," a name her students lovingly called her. Today Bethune-Cookman College stands as a living, growing monument to a woman who started with $1.50 and a dream.

Young women at Bethune-Cookman College in the 1940s

Plot

- A story's **plot** includes the important events that happen in the beginning, middle, and end of a story.

- Look for events that are important to the plot. They help keep the story going.

- A story map can help you keep track of the most important events in a story.

Read "Chiefy Stays Over" from *Popsicle Pony* by Jill Stover.

Write About It

1. Make a story map with a classmate. Write *beginning* at the top of a piece of paper, *middle* in the middle of the paper, and *end* near the bottom of the paper.

2. Write important events that happen in each part of the story. Share your map.

Chiefy Stays Over

by Jill Stover

A girl decides to help out the owner of a pony-drawn ice cream wagon by taking care of his pony, Chiefy.

One evening Popsicle Pete didn't come. He was sick and had to go to the hospital for a few days. Chiefy came to stay with me. My backyard became a real Texas ranch, and I turned into a real Texas cowgirl.

Every morning I tried to ride Chiefy over to the hospital to see Popsicle Pete. And every morning he refused to go. I coaxed him with carrots. I bribed him with cookies. I even tried chili peppers. But Chiefy was stubborn, and I didn't know how to handle him. He wouldn't budge.

I went out to try one more time. The yard was empty. Chiefy had escaped. Pretty soon we got a call from the county sheriff. Chiefy was in big trouble.

After his great escape, he had taken his regular route through town. First he went to the Moo-Moo to get a special treat. Then he went past the Longhorn Feed Store for another little something. Finally he stopped at the Twin Dophins Movie Theater for one more snack. The movie must have been pretty exciting, because Chiefy decided to stay. But he raised a ruckus, and the manager called in the sheriff.

When he was arrested, Chiefy trotted happily along his regular route to the county jail, where he was locked in a cell to keep him out of any more trouble.

LOOK AHEAD

In *Leah's Pony*, Leah is proud of her pony. All seems fine until real trouble starts. Read and see what important events happen in the beginning, middle, and end of the story.

Vocabulary

Words to Know

chores	pasture	sturdy
pony	swift	dust
saddle		

Words with similar meanings, such as *happy* and *joyful,* are **synonyms.** You can often figure out the meaning of an unknown word by looking for a clue around it. This clue is sometimes a synonym.

Read the paragraph. Notice how *jobs* helps you understand *chores.*

Work Some, Play Some

Lucia watched the dust blowing around the cornfields, but weeding was one of the many jobs she had to do. Only after her chores were done could she play. As she worked, Lucia thought of her pony Freckles. She saw the sturdy, swift animal out in the pasture running here and there. She couldn't wait to get into the saddle and ride him again.

Talk About It

What things would you like to do on a farm? Tell a friend. Use as many vocabulary words as you can.

Leah's Pony

written by Elizabeth Friedrich

illustrated by Michael Garland

The year the corn grew tall and straight, Leah's papa bought her a pony. The pony was strong and swift and sturdy, with just a snip of white at the end of his soft black nose. Papa taught Leah to place her new saddle right in the middle of his back and tighten the girth around his belly, just so.

That whole summer, Leah and her pony crossed through cloud-capped cornfields and chased cattle through the pasture.

Leah scratched that special spot under her pony's mane and brushed him till his coat glistened like satin.

Each day Leah loved to ride her pony into town just to hear Mr. B. shout from the door of his grocery store, "That's the finest pony in the whole county."

The year the corn grew no taller than a man's thumb, Leah's house became very quiet. Sometimes on those hot, dry nights, Leah heard Papa and Mama's hushed voices whispering in the kitchen. She couldn't understand the words but knew their sad sound.

Some days the wind blew so hard it turned the sky black with dust. It was hard for Leah to keep her pony's coat shining. It was hard for Mama to keep the house clean. It was hard for Papa to carry buckets of water for the sow and her piglets.

Soon Papa sold the pigs and even some of the cattle. "These are hard times," he told Leah with a puzzled look. "That's what these days are, all right, hard times."

Mama used flour sacks to make underwear for
Leah. Mama threw dishwater on her drooping
petunias to keep them growing. And, no matter
what else happened, Mama always woke Leah
on Saturday with the smell of fresh, hot coffee
cake baking.

One hot, dry, dusty day grasshoppers turned
the day to night. They ate the trees bare and left
only twigs behind.

The next day the neighbors filled their truck
with all they owned and stopped to say good-bye.
"We're off to Oregon," they said. "It must be better
there." Papa, Mama, and Leah waved as their
neighbors wobbled down the road in an old truck
overflowing with chairs and bedsprings and wire.

The hot, dry, dusty days kept coming. On a day you could almost taste the earth in the air, Papa said, "I have something to tell you, Leah, and I want you to be brave. I borrowed money from the bank, I bought seeds, but the seeds dried up and blew away. Nothing grew. I don't have any corn to sell. Now I can't pay back the bank," Papa paused. "They're going to have an auction, Leah. They're going to sell the cattle and the chickens and the pickup truck."

Leah stared at Papa. His voice grew husky and soft. "Worst of all, they're going to sell my tractor.

I'll never be able to plant corn when she's gone.
Without my tractor, we might even have to leave
the farm. I told you, Leah, these are hard times."

Leah knew what an auction meant. She knew
eager faces with strange voices would come to
their farm. They would stand outside and offer
money for Papa's best bull and Mama's prize
rooster and Leah's favorite calf.

All week Leah worried and waited and
wondered what to do. One morning she watched
as a man in a big hat hammered a sign into the
ground in front of her house.

Leah wanted to run away. She raced her pony past empty fields lined with dry gullies. She galloped past a house with rags stuffed in broken windowpanes. She sped right past Mr. B. sweeping the steps outside his store.

At last Leah knew what she had to do. She turned her pony around and rode back into town.

She stopped in front of Mr. B.'s store. "You can buy my pony," she said.

Mr. B. stopped sweeping and stared at her. "Why would you want to sell him?" he asked. "That's the finest pony in the county."

Leah swallowed hard. "I've grown a lot this summer," she said. "I'm getting too big for him."

Sunburned soil crunched under Leah's feet as she walked home alone. The auction had begun. Neighbors, friends, strangers—everyone clustered around the man in the big hat. "How much for this wagon?" boomed the man. "Five dollars. Ten dollars. Sold for fifteen dollars to the man in the green shirt."

Papa's best bull.

Sold.

Mama's prize rooster.

Sold.

Leah's favorite calf.

Sold.

Leah clutched her money in her hand. "It has to be enough," she whispered to herself. "It just has to be."

"Here's one of the best items in this entire auction," yelled the man in the big hat. "Who'll start the bidding at five hundred dollars for this practically new, all-purpose Farmall tractor? It'll plow, plant, fertilize, and even cultivate for you."

It was time. Leah's voice shook. "One dollar."

The man in the big hat laughed. "That's a low starting bid if I ever heard one," he said. "Now let's hear some serious bids."

No one moved. No one said a word. No one even seemed to breathe.

"Ladies and gentlemen, this tractor is a beauty! I have a bid of only one dollar for it. One dollar for this practically new Farmall tractor! Do I hear any other bids?"

Again no one moved. No one said a word. No one even seemed to breathe.

"This is ridiculous!" the man's voice boomed out from under his hat into the silence. "Sold to the young lady for one dollar."

The crowd cheered. Papa's mouth hung open. Mama cried. Leah proudly walked up and handed one dollar to the auctioneer in the big hat.

"That young lady bought one fine tractor for one very low price," the man continued. "Now how much am I bid for this flock of healthy young chickens?"

"I'll give you ten cents," offered a farmer who lived down the road.

"Ten cents! Ten cents is mighty cheap for a whole flock of chickens," the man said. His face looked angry.

Again no one moved. No one said a word. No one even seemed to breathe.

"Sold for ten cents!"

The farmer picked up the cage filled with chickens and walked over to Mama. "These chickens are yours," he said.

The man pushed his big hat back on his head. "How much for this good Ford pickup truck?" he asked.

"Twenty-five cents," yelled a neighbor from town.

Again no one moved. No one said a word. No one even seemed to breathe.

"Sold for twenty-five cents!" The man in the big hat shook his head. "This isn't supposed to be a penny auction!" he shouted.

The neighbor paid his twenty-five cents and took the keys to the pickup truck. "I think these will start your truck," he whispered as he dropped the keys into Papa's shirt pocket.

Leah watched as friends and neighbors bid a penny for a chicken or a nickel for a cow or a quarter for a plow. One by one, they gave everything back to Mama and Papa.

The crowds left. The sign disappeared. Chickens scratched in their coop, and cattle called for their corn. The farm was quiet. Too quiet. No familiar whinny greeted Leah when she entered the barn. Leah swallowed hard and straightened her back.

That night in Leah's hushed house, no sad voices whispered in the kitchen. Only Leah lay awake, listening to the clock chime nine and even ten times. Leah's heart seemed to copy its slow, sad beat.

The next morning Leah forced open the heavy
barn doors to start her chores. A loud whinny
greeted her. Leah ran and hugged the familiar
furry neck and kissed the white snip of a nose.
"You're back!" she cried. "How did you get here?"

Then Leah saw the note with her name written in big letters:

Dear Leah,

    This is the finest pony in the county. But he's a little bit small for me and a little bit big for my grandson.

        He fits you much better.

                Your friend,

                Mr. B.

P.S. I heard how you saved your family's farm. These hard times won't last forever.

And they didn't.

About the Author

Elizabeth Friedrich

Elizabeth Friedrich knows what farm life is like. She lives in Stratham, New Hampshire, with her husband and her two children. They share their farm with six sheep and a horse named Tuffy.

Reader Response

Open for Discussion

Pretend you are Leah telling your grandchildren about the pony you once owned and the hard times you lived through.

Comprehension Check

1. Why did Leah offer only one dollar for the tractor? Use details to support you answer.

2. "Hard times" are an important part of the setting of the story. What are some story details that make that time come to life for you?

3. How does the picture on page 259 help you know how brave Leah is?

4. Write the three most important events of the **plot** that tell the beginning, middle, and end of the story. (Plot)

5. Which of these events is more important to the **plot** of *Leah's Pony?* Tell why. (Plot)
- The neighbors pack up and leave.
- Leah sells her pony.

Test Prep

Look Back and Write

Look back through the story. What kind of person was Leah at the beginning of the story? How did she change in the middle and end? Use pictures and text to support your answer.

Giddyap!

by Sarah Bourdelais

Would you like to learn how to ride a horse? You can, if you're seven or older. You can take lessons at a riding stable. The only things you need to bring with you are boots with heels (no tennis shoes!) and a riding hat.

Once you're up on a horse, what do you do? You learn how to sit in the saddle. Your backbone must be right above the horse's backbone. Otherwise, you might fall off.

Sit up straight from your head to your hips. Look straight ahead to watch where you're going. Relax your shoulders and let your upper arms hang loosely at your sides.

Hold the reins in front of you, a few inches above the horse's back. Your hands should be fists with your thumbs on top. Are your feet in the stirrups? Good! Make sure your heels are pointing down.

Practice sitting on a horse by using a chair or a large pillow at home. Better yet, do you have a barrel? It's shaped like a horse's body.

After you start sitting on a horse correctly, you'll learn how to talk to the horse. You'll talk, not just with words, but also with your weight, your legs, and the reins.

Do you want the horse to move forward? Lean forward, but not too much. Push your feet down into the stirrups and squeeze the horse's body with your legs. Say "walk" or "giddyap." Don't pull on the reins. It will confuse the horse. By leaning, squeezing a little, and saying the right word, the horse should move forward.

To turn right, twist your upper body to the right. Pull gently on the right rein and shift your weight to the same side. Don't bend at the waist or move your hips.

English Riding Equipment

Are you ready to stop? Pull on the reins and say, "Whoa!"

With a lot of practice, you can be an expert rider. Happy trails!

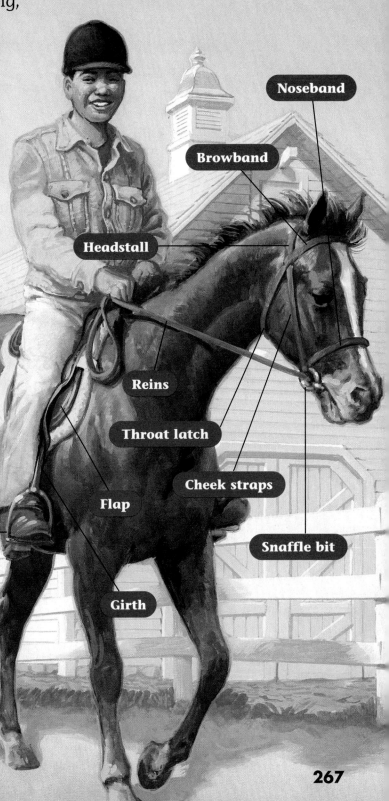

Noseband

Browband

Headstall

Reins

Pad

Throat latch

Cheek straps

Flap

Stirrup

Snaffle bit

Girth

Poetry

At the Library

by Nikki Grimes

I flip the pages of a book and slip inside,
where crystal seas await and pirates hide.
I find a paradise where birds can talk,
where children fly and trees prefer to walk.
Sometimes I end up on a city street.
I recognize the brownskin girl I meet.
She's skinny, but she's strong, and brave, and wise.
I smile because I see me in her eyes.

A Book

by Myra Cohn Livingston

Closed, I am a mystery.
Open, I will always be
a friend with whom you think and see.

Closed, there's nothing I can say.
Open, we can dream and stray
to other worlds, far and away.

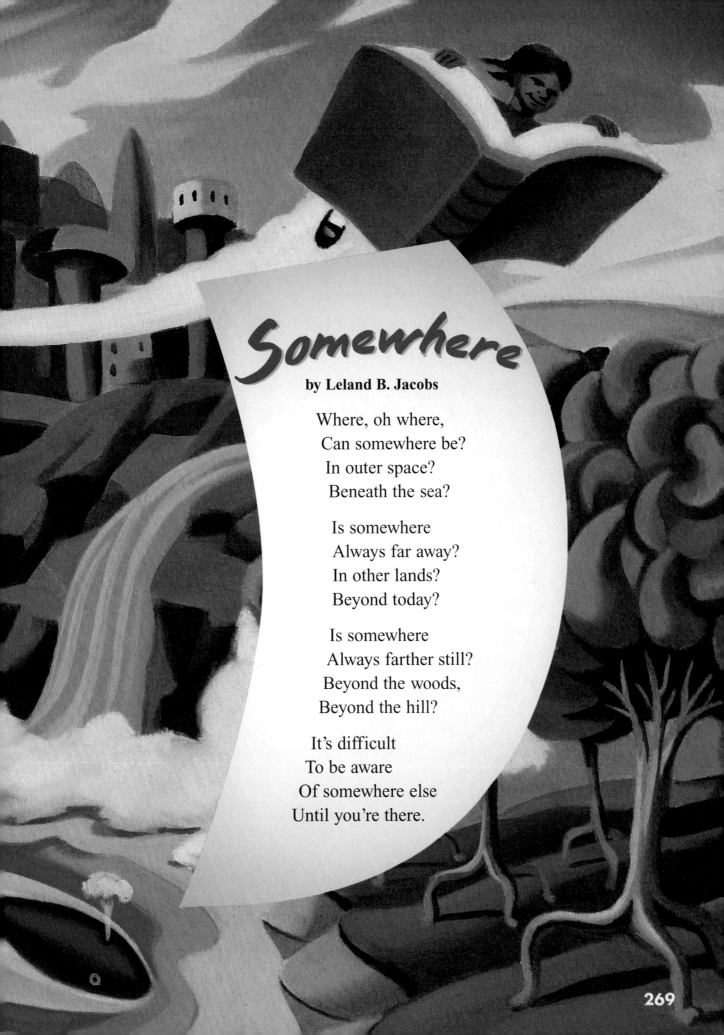

Somewhere

by Leland B. Jacobs

Where, oh where,
Can somewhere be?
In outer space?
Beneath the sea?

Is somewhere
Always far away?
In other lands?
Beyond today?

Is somewhere
Always farther still?
Beyond the woods,
Beyond the hill?

It's difficult
To be aware
Of somewhere else
Until you're there.

LET'S SEND A ROCKET

by Kit Patrickson

Ten, nine, eight . . .
Seven, six, five . . .

We'll send up a rocket,
And it will be *live*.

Five, four, three . . .
It's ready to zoom!

We're counting each second,
And soon it will boom!

Get ready for . . . two;
Get ready to go . . .

It's *two*—and it's—*one*—
We're OFF! It's ZERO!

The Moon, a Banana

by Jesús Carlos Soto Morfín

A banana left
at night
on a plane

Since then
he's been stuck
in the sky
and we call him moon

Wrap-Up

How can visits to other times and other places make our lives better?

All Aboard!

Make a Travel Poster

In this unit, you travel to other times and places. Work with a partner to convince others that they can learn from a journey to a new destination.

1. **Choose** a time and place from a selection in this unit.

2. **Make** a travel poster to convince others to join you in a journey to this destination. Include information about whom they will meet and what they will learn.

Dear Diary

Write a Diary Entry

In *Flight: The Journey of Charles Lindbergh,* Lindbergh "keeps a diary as he goes all day long, hour by hour. It is as if he were speaking to himself."

1. **Choose** a journey from this unit to write about.

2. **Reread** the selection and imagine being part of what happens hour by hour.

3. **Write** a diary entry for one day of the journey. Write as if you are speaking to yourself.

Picture This!

Create a Photo Album

In *Chibi: A True Story from Japan,* photographers took pictures of Chibi and her family. Imagine you are the photographer for one of the selections in this unit.

1. **Look over** your selection. List the events that best tell the story.

2. **Draw** a "photo" for each event and write a caption to explain it.

3. **Create** a photo album. Place the photos in order and design a cover.

Let's Talk

Conduct an Interview

Both Irene in *Brave Irene* and Leah in *Leah's Pony* were heroes who helped their families.

1. **Choose** one of these heroes to interview. You and your partner can choose to be the host or the hero.

2. **Write** interview questions. Practice asking the questions and listening to the answers.

3. **Conduct** the interview for others.

Test Talk

Answer the Question

Write the Answer

Tests often tell you to write an answer. A test about "$1.50 and a Dream," pages 244–245, might have this question.

Test Question 1

Why did the author name this selection "$1.50 and a Dream"? Use details from the selection to support your answer.

Get ready to answer.

- Find key words in the question.

- Finish the statement "I need to find out . . ."

- Decide where to look.

- Make notes on details.

Write your answer.

- Begin your answer with words from the question. Then include details from your notes.

- Check your answer. Ask yourself:

  ✓ **Is my answer correct?** Are some details incorrect?

  ✓ **Is my answer complete?** Do I need to add more details?

  ✓ **Is my answer focused?** Do all my details come from the text? Do they all help answer the question?

See how one student writes a correct, complete, and focused response.

I'll start my answer with these words from the question: "The author named this selection '$1.50 and a Dream' because . . ." Now I'll get the rest of the answer from my notes.

The author named this selection "$1.50 and a Dream" because she wants us to remember that even though Mary McLeod Bethune achieved great things, she started out with only $1.50 and a dream of . . .

Try it!

Now write correct, complete, and focused responses to these test questions about "$1.50 and a Dream," pages 244–245.

Test Question 2
Where did Ms. Bethune get what she needed to start her school? Use details from the selection to explain your answer.

Test Question 3
What happened after Ms. Bethune's school combined with Cookman Institute? Use details from the selection to support your answer.

Imagination.
kids

How many ways
can we use our
imaginations?

Skill Lesson

Steps in a Process

- Following **steps in a process** usually means doing or making something in a certain order. The steps might show the best way to make or do something.

- Sometimes the steps are given in pictures as well as words.

- Sometimes there are clue words, such as *the next step* or *then*, that help you with the order of the steps.

Read "Revealing a Pattern" from *Drawing: A Young Artist's Guide* by Jude Welton.

TATE GALLERY
Drawing
A young artist's guide

Jude Welton

Talk About It

1. Each numbered step in "Revealing a Pattern" has more than one direction. Why do you think the author wrote the steps this way?

2. Do you think it would be easier to make each step one statement? Why or why not?

Revealing a Pattern
by Jude Welton

You can find patterns all around you, in both natural objects such as feathers, leaves, and shells, and manufactured objects, like fabrics, tiles, and carpets. Even your own skin has a pattern if you look closely. Sometimes a pattern is made up of lines only and sometimes it is made up of different colored shapes. Every object has its own texture, too, which you can see as well as touch. Think about the way patterns and textures combine on the surface of objects, and how you can use these combinations in your drawings.

Find a leaf with a strong vein pattern. You can make a copy of it by taking a rubbing.

1. Place the leaf smooth side down. Lay a sheet of paper over the leaf and rub over it firmly with a wax crayon. Its outline and the pattern of the veins should come clear.

2. Use different colored crayons to make leaf rubbings all over the paper. Go over the lines with colored pencil to strengthen the pattern.

3. You can brush a thin coat of watercolor over your repeat design. The wax crayon will hold off the watercolor so that the full leaf pattern stands out against the background.

LOOK AHEAD

The Piñata Maker

written and photographed by George Ancona

In *The Piñata Maker,* Tío Rico makes piñatas for a living. Read and follow the steps as he turns paper into a beautiful swan.

Vocabulary

Many words have more than one meaning. To decide which meaning of a word is being used, look for clues in the surrounding sentences.

Read the paragraph below. Decide if *cone* means "an object with a flat, round base and pointed top" or "a scaly growth that bears the seeds on many evergreen trees."

Designing Decorations

I <u>designed</u> a beautiful <u>swan</u> out of papier-mâché for a party decoration. <u>Creating</u> the graceful long-necked bird was easy. I mixed sticky <u>paste</u> with water and soaked newspaper strips in it. Then I formed the newspaper strips into a <u>cone</u>. Finally, I shaped the cone into a swan. Maybe someday I will be <u>famous</u> for my creations!

Write About It

Write directions for a craft project that you enjoy. Use as many vocabulary words as you can.

The
Piñata
Maker

written and photographed

by George Ancona

Don Ricardo is seventy-seven years old. He started creating piñatas fifteen years ago when his former job, making felt sombreros, became too hard for him. "I went to school," he says. "But I didn't learn very much. I liked to go to the river and play with my friends until one of our fathers would discover us and chase us back to school. My father was a hatter, and I left school to help him. After I married I started my own hat business.

"I think that working all those years in front of the hot fire gave me the rheumatism," he continues, moving about the house with the help of a cane. "It gave me the money to build this house brick by brick, but it also made it hard for me to walk."

Don Ricardo starts his day by making paste in the kitchen. He puts a small handful of flour into an old pot, adds enough water to make a thin paste, and breaks apart the lumps with his fingers. He adds kindling to the fire and fans it until the flames leap up. Then he puts the pot on the fire and stirs the mixture until it thickens. "Starch makes a better paste than flour," says Don Ricardo, "but it is scarce in town and very expensive."

Today Tío Rico is making a piñata in the shape of a swan. He begins by rolling dry banana leaves into a thick rod with a bulge at one end for the head. He wraps the rod in brown paper smeared with paste. Then he forms the neck into an S-shaped curve and places it in the sun. Old irons hold it in shape until it's dry.

Next Tío Rico covers the neck with white paper so the brown won't show through the outer layer of white crepe paper feathers. Then he makes a shallow cardboard cone, cuts it in the center, and glues it onto the base of the neck.

Tío Rico rolls another piece of cardboard into a large cone. He bends the ends to form the swan's tail and wraps it.

Using a pattern he designed, Tío Rico traces the shape of the wings onto cardboard and cuts them out. He covers these with paper too.

Next he cuts out two cardboard triangles and bends them in the middle to form the swan's beak. Then he cuts out the feet, making them look as if they are paddling. These he also covers with paper.

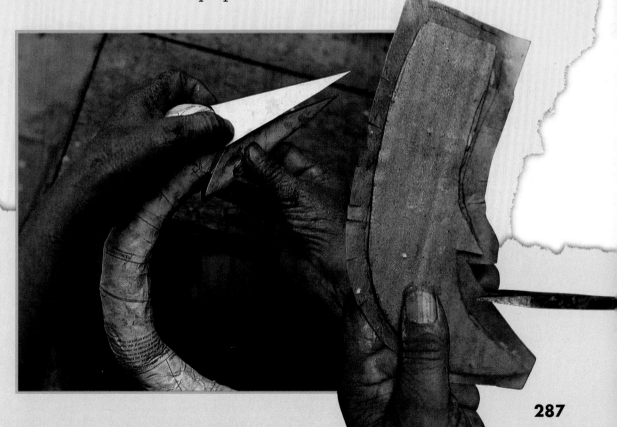

Then Tío Rico makes the swan's eyes, cutting out circles from the black letters on the cement bag. He pastes one circle on each side of the head.

Tío Rico needs some pots for his piñatas. So he puts on his hat, takes up his cane, and sets off for the market. There he finds the two pots he needs, one larger than the other.

Back home Tío Rico ties some strong twine around the neck of the smaller pot, leaving some loose to form a handle.

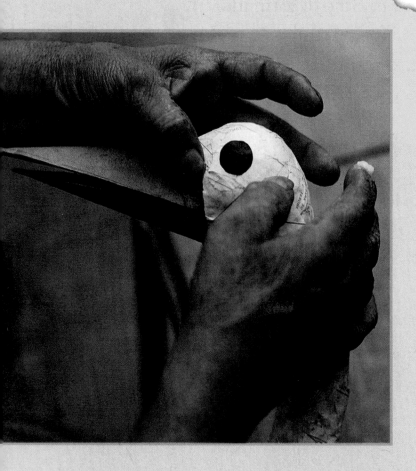

In order to keep the swan's body round, he cuts off the collar of the pot, then glues newspaper all over the pot and the string.

Next come the feathers. Using pinking shears, Tío Rico snips into a folded strip of white crepe paper and wraps it with glue onto the tail.

Then he pastes the neck and tail onto the body.

He paints the beak yellow and the feet orange.
After pasting the feet into position, Tío Rico adds
more feathers to the body and wings of the swan.

When everything is dry, Tío Rico uses a nail to
poke two small holes through the wings and the
pot. With a large needle and strong thread, he
secures the wings to the body.

Tío Rico covers the knotted threads with more white crepe paper feathers and holds up the swan for inspection. "Well," he says, pleased with his work, "let's see who will break this one."

Another of Tío Rico's famous piñatas is ready for a fiesta.

A Note from the Author/Photographer
George Ancona

My children, Lisa, Gina, Tomás, Isabel, Marina, and Pablo, all enjoyed breaking piñatas at their parties. We did not have a market where we could buy pots to make the piñatas, so we used cardboard boxes, which we made into shapes and then covered with paper. You can also use inflated balloons covered with papier-mâché. When the paper is dry, paint it, then cut a hole to fill the piñata with goodies.

Reader Response

Now that you know how Don Ricardo makes a swan piñata, tell how you would make a piñata for a birthday party. What shape would you make?

Comprehension Check

1. Does Don Ricardo take pride in his work? Use details from the selection to support your answer.

2. Look back at the selection. Which helps you more to understand how a piñata is made—the text or the photographs? Why?

3. Look back at the selection. Then make a chart with two columns. One column should list the tools and the other should list the materials Don Ricardo uses to make his piñatas.

4. What is the first **step in the process** Don Ricardo takes to make a piñata? (Steps in a Process)

5. What is the next **step in the process** after Don Ricardo cuts the collar off the pot? (Steps in a Process)

Test Prep
Look Back and Write

An author writes to inform, to express or describe, to persuade, or to entertain. Why did this author write about a piñata maker? Use information from the selection to support your answer.

Southwest Settlements

from Grade 3, Silver Burdett Ginn
Communities Around Us
Social Studies Program

Test Prep

How to Read a Textbook Lesson

1. Preview

- A textbook lesson is organized to help you learn and remember certain ideas and facts. Look at the title, headings, and time line. What other parts will help you learn?

2. Read and Use Text Features

- Before you read, go to "Think About It" at the end of the lesson. Find the answer as you read the text.

- You may find information you need on the time line.

3. Think and Connect

Think about *The Piñata Maker.* Then look over your notes from "Southwest Settlements."

Tío Rico comes to your school to tell you about piñatas. Tell him about other examples of Spanish culture you see around you.

The Spanish Southwest

The Spaniards came to the Americas in search of gold and silver. Spanish soldiers conquered the Aztecs of Mexico in 1521. Spanish explorers pushed northward during the 1500s, claiming more and more land for Spain. Soon, Spain began to set up colonies in the present-day states of Florida, New Mexico, Texas, and California.

Missions and Forts

Spanish settlers, priests, and soldiers from Mexico arrived in New

Today this mission is part of the San Antonio Missions National Park in Texas.

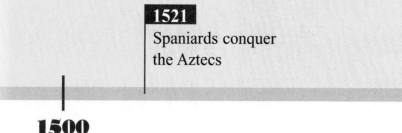

1521
Spaniards conquer
the Aztecs

1598
Spanish settlers arrive
in New Mexico

1500   **1600**

This painting shows cowboys working on a ranch.

Mexico in 1598. By 1690 there was a mission in Texas. In 1769 the Spaniards had a mission in California. The priests started missions to teach their religion to Native Americans. The soldiers built presidios, or forts, to defend the missions.

The First Ranches

Some settlers in the Spanish Southwest lived in farming villages or in towns. Many people lived on ranches and raised cattle, horses, and sheep. The workers hired to care for these animals were called **vaqueros** (vä ke′ rōz). *Vaquero* comes from the Spanish word *vaca,* which means "cow." Much of the clothes and equipment of the vaquero were later used by cowboys of the American West.

Ranching was important to the Spanish Southwest. The livestock raised on ranches supplied the nearby missions, villages, and towns with food, leather, and tallow, or animal fat used in making candles and soap.

Spanish Culture

If you were to travel through the southwestern United States today, you would see many ways in which Spanish culture has become a part of the culture of the United States.

Many place names, including *Montana* and *Nevada,* came from the Spanish language. Some rivers in Texas, such as the *Rio Grande* and the *Brazos,* also have Spanish names.

vaquero a person who cares for cattle, horses, or sheep

1690
First Spanish
mission in Texas

1769
First Spanish
mission in California

1700

1800

American cowboys still practice the skills of roping and herding cattle learned from Mexican cowboys. Many cowboy terms, such as *ranch* and *lasso,* come from the Spanish language.

The Spanish style of building also found a home in the Southwest. Here many beautiful buildings have tan walls of **adobe,** a type of hardened clay.

The Indians in Mexico taught the Spaniards to use tomatoes, corn, and many types of beans. Together the Spaniards and the Indians of Mexico have given us tortillas, chili, and tacos.

adobe a clay brick that has dried in the sun

This photo shows an adobe building.

Show What You Know

Refocus
In what parts of the American Southwest did Spaniards settle?

Think About It
Give an example of a Spanish contribution to the culture of our country and explain its importance.

Community Check
Look at a map of your community and make a list of place names. Do some research to find out what language some of the place names come from.

Skill Lesson

Setting

- The **setting** is the time and place of a story.

- An author may not always tell you when and where a story takes place. Look for clues in the art or words that point to the setting of a story.

- The setting can have an effect on how a character acts in a story.

Read "On the Train" from *Bonanza Girl* by Patricia Beatty.

Talk About It

1. When do you think this story takes place? Why do you think so?

2. Does the setting have any effect on how the main character acts? Why do you think this way?

Patricia Beatty
BONANZA GIRL

On the Train

by Patricia Beatty

When train time was called, we marched right past the bulging eyes of the ticket agent and took our places in the railroad car. "Well, we're on our way, children," Mama called. "You try to sleep as much as you can, so we won't be too tired when we come to Spokane Falls, and Jemmy, you keep away from doors and the stove and kerosene lamps, and do obey the conductor."

While Mama gave Jemmy instructions he certainly had no intention of following, I looked around the railroad car and sighed. It was like every other car I'd ever seen. The seats were hard and uncomfortable and about as slick as an icy hill, and every time I squirmed a little I nearly fell off into the aisle. There were kerosene lanterns hanging from the roof, and there was a coal and wood stove at the opposite end of the car. I took off my bonnet and gloves, placed my traveling cloak on the back of the seat, and settled down as best I could.

The train followed the Columbia River, and we stared out the windows at the great rock cliffs and waterfalls, but once we left the banks of the river, there was almost nothing to see. We rode for miles and miles and hours and hours, and saw nothing at all but dry prairie land, spotted here and there with sagebrush and sand dunes. When we came to a dusty little place called Wallula, we all switched to a new Northern Pacific line, finished two years before. While our baggage was moved, Mama, Jemmy, and I crossed the tracks along with the other passengers to have a cup of tea at a dusty little restaurant.

LOOK AHEAD

In *Mailing May*, a little girl wants to go visit her grandmother in another part of the state. Read to see if you can tell when and where this story takes place.

Vocabulary

Words to Know

bundled	**label**	**mailing**
conductor	**carted**	**station**

Many words have more than one meaning. To decide which meaning of a word is being used, look for clues in nearby sentences.

Read the paragraph below. Decide if *conductor* means "a thing that transmits heat" or "a person in charge of a train and its passengers."

A Package for Larry

I like <u>mailing</u> packages to my brother Larry, who lives across the country. I <u>bundled</u> some cookies and put them in a box. Then I attached a <u>label</u> with Larry's address. My mom drove me to the train <u>station</u>. I watched as a forklift <u>carted</u> my package with hundreds of others to a waiting train. With the packages loaded, the <u>conductor</u>, the man in charge, signaled, and the cookies were on their way!

Talk About It

Imagine you are a package. Describe your journey from one place to another. Use vocabulary words.

MAILING MAY

MICHAEL O. TUNNELL

ILLUSTRATED BY

TED RAND

It all started when Ma and Pa promised I could stay a spell with Grandma Mary, who lived a million miles away through the rough old Idaho mountains. But when I asked Ma if it was time to go, she just shook her head and sighed real deep. So I tried asking Pa.

"No money," said Pa. "Train ticket costs a dollar fifty-five, May. I work all day to make that much. Maybe next year."

But I just couldn't wait a whole year! So the next morning when Ma bundled me in my heavy winter coat and sent me out to play in the snow, I made a beeline for Alexander's Department Store. Mr. Alexander called his hello from atop a ladder.

"I need a job," I said. "I need money for the train."

Mr. Alexander smiled as he stepped down to the floor. "A job, is it? I wish I could hire you, May, but all the jobs around here are grown-up jobs, like counting money and lifting heavy cartons."

I must have looked mighty sad, because Mr. Alexander reached for a jar of peppermint sticks. The sweet, wintry taste didn't do much to cheer me as I slogged my way home.

Things only got worse when Pa came back from work that night. He and Ma commenced to whispering and peeking at me off and on.

Then they made me go to bed awful early, which I did not like at all.

Next morning Ma shook me awake while it was still real dark. I was puzzled to see Pa's little traveling bag, packed and standing by the door. When I asked where he was going, Ma only smiled and said, "Eat your breakfast."

Just then someone knocked on our front door. Pa opened up to Ma's cousin Leonard.

"Come along, May," Pa said, grabbing the suitcase as Ma helped me with my coat. "We're going to the post office with Leonard." He held up his hand as I opened my mouth. "No questions," Pa said with a wink.

Ma hugged and kissed me before Pa took my hand and led me out into the dark winter air.

Before long I stood taking in the funny smells of the Grangeville post office: glue and canvas bags and oiled wooden floors. Meanwhile, Pa marched right up to Postmaster Perkins and said, "Sam, you got some new rules for mailing packages. I know boxes can weigh up to fifty pounds nowadays. But what sorts of things can you send?"

Mr. Perkins looked at Pa real strange-like as he asked, "What you got in mind, John?"

"It's May," said Pa. "We'd like to mail her to Lewiston. Leonard here mans the mail car on the train, as you well know. He can take good care of our package."

305

"Sure thing, Sam," said Leonard.

I was flat flabbergasted by Pa, and so was Mr. Perkins. "Mailing May?" he mumbled, shaking his head.

"Let's see. The postal code says not to mail lizards or insects or anything smelly." Mr. Perkins looked at me over his glasses and then sniffed. "Guess you pass the smell test."

"But what about girls?" I asked. "Can you mail me?"

"Well, the rule book says nothing about children, but it is permissible to mail baby chicks." Mr. Perkins smiled. "Let's find out exactly how much you and your valise weigh."

I scrambled up onto the big scale, and Pa set his traveling bag next to me.

"Forty-eight pounds and eight ounces. Biggest baby chick on record!" Mr. Perkins ran his finger down a chart hanging near the scale and turned to Pa. "To mail May from Grangeville to Lewiston will cost fifty-three cents. Well, Leonard, looks like you'll be in charge of some poultry on this mail run."

Before I knew it, Mr. Perkins had glued fifty-three cents worth of stamps on the back of my coat, along with a label that read:

Mrs. C. G. Vennigerholz
1156 Twelfth Ave
Lewiston, Idaho

DELIVER TO

Pa hugged me and told me to be good for Grandma Mary. Then he was gone, and there I was, a package sitting in the post office. Before long, Leonard carted me and the rest of the mail to the train station. The big black steam engine was already waiting, hissing and snorting like a boar hog. The sight made me go all tingly, seeing as I'd never ever ridden on a train before.

After Leonard loaded the mailbags and a few other packages, he called out, "Time to go, May." Then he helped me up the steel steps.

At exactly seven o'clock, the train chugged away from my home and headed down the mountain. I felt as adventuresome as Daniel Boone!

The inside of the mail car was like a little post office, and Leonard got busy right away sorting mail to be dropped off at towns along the way. I curled up nearby the stove to keep warm and watched.

Whenever Leonard had a free minute, he'd take me to the door for a look. My, oh, my, what sights there were to see! Why, we hung on the edge of mountainsides and crawled through tunnels. We crossed deep valleys on top of tall, spidery trestles that Leonard called "steel on stilts."

Then long about Lapwai Canyon, where the train track twists back and forth down the mountain, I began to feel somewhat less adventuresome. Instead, I was feeling dizzy and weak in the stomach. I was about to run to get some fresh air when I heard an angry voice at the door.

"Leonard," yelled a man in a uniform, "that girl better have a ticket or money to buy one."

It was Mr. Harry Morris, the train's conductor. I hid behind Leonard as he explained that I was a package, not a passenger. Then he showed Mr. Morris the stamps on my coat. That cranky old conductor slapped his knee and laughed out loud.

"I've seen everything now," said Mr. Morris, wiping his eyes.

Well, Mr. Morris plumb scared the dizziness right out of me! Even my stomach seemed better, and I started feeling hungry. Leonard said lunch would be at Grandma Mary's.

The train made a few more stops at towns like Sweetwater and Joseph before we pulled into the Lewiston railroad station. Since this was the end of the line, Leonard had time to be my mail carrier, and we headed for Grandma Mary's place.

The second I laid eyes on Grandma Mary, I felt downright warm inside. Ma and Pa had kept their promise after all—with a little help from the U.S. Post Office!

About the Author

When Michael O. Tunnell heard a teacher reading a story to a group of students, he knew he wanted to write children's books. Mr. Tunnell thought he would write fantasy stories, but most of his stories are about real events. "I'm just fascinated when it comes to history," he said. "It's important to show history is made up of stories of all of the rest of us, not just famous people."

Mr. Tunnell lives in Utah and teaches college students about children's literature. He and his wife, Glenna, have four children and one grandchild.

FRAGILE

TED RAND

About the Illustrator

Ted Rand also illustrated the book *Knots on a Counting Rope* by Bill Martin, Jr., and John Archambault. Mr. Rand has lived in Washington state all his life, except for the four years he spent in the Navy.

316

Reader Response

Open for Discussion

Pretend that you can walk into the illustrations for *Mailing May*. As you stand in each picture, look around. What do you see, hear, smell, and feel?

Comprehension Check

1. May's feelings change during the story. Name three feelings that May has. Use details to support your answer.

2. The story takes place a long time ago, and the author helps us see this by using some old-fashioned expressions— words and phrases that we may know, but that we don't use much today. Make a list of old-fashioned expressions from the story and tell what they mean.

3. The families in both *Mailing May* and *Leah's Pony* talk about hard times. Which family seems to be having the worse time? Use details to support your answer.

4. The **setting** of *Mailing May* is 1914 in Idaho. What details in the story and pictures tell you that this story takes place a long time ago? (Setting)

5. If the **setting** of the story were today, how would the story be different? (Setting)

 Test Prep

Look Back and Write

Why didn't May sit with other passengers on the train? How was she different from them? Use details from the story to support your answer.

317

Early Mail Delivery

by John Coiley

IN THE 1800s some steam engines pulled mail cars that were designed to handle all the jobs carried out in a post office while the train sped along. The mail was picked up from a trackside pouch. Mail clerks then sorted and put it into sacks for different destinations along the train's route. These sacks were automatically dropped off into trackside nets.

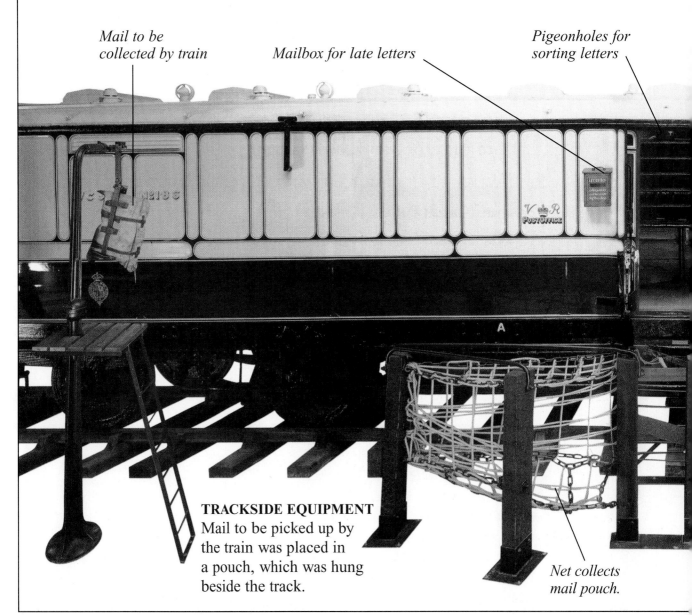

Mail to be collected by train

Mailbox for late letters

Pigeonholes for sorting letters

TRACKSIDE EQUIPMENT
Mail to be picked up by the train was placed in a pouch, which was hung beside the track.

Net collects mail pouch.

ROAD TO RAIL

Sending mail by rail requires cooperation between the railroads and local postal services. Here, the mail car delivers mail to a branch-line station. The local train then takes the mail to a mail-line station, where it is put aboard a long-distance passenger train or Traveling Post Office train.

WHAT GOES WHERE?

Incoming mail was emptied from the sacks onto the sorting table, and individual letters were hand sorted into pigeonholes. When there were enough letters for one destination, they were tied in a bundle and put in a sack. The sack was dropped off along the way or at the end of the journey.

Net picks up mail bag from lineside.

AMERICAN MAIL

This classic American locomotive from the 1870s is hauling a mail train.

British Traveling
Post Office car, 1885

Leather bag with sorted mail to be dropped off

POST OFFICE ON WHEELS

In 1838, with the arrival of a regular railroad passenger service in Britain, it was decided that the mail should be carried by rail. In the U.S., the first Railway Post Office came into operation in 1864. The railroads are still used today by mail services around the world, along with road and air transport.

Visualizing

- To **visualize** is to create a picture in your mind.

- You can put yourself into the story or article by using all your senses when you read.

- When you read, you may be able to use details in the text along with what you know about the subject to see, hear, smell, taste, and feel what the author describes.

Read "First Day in London" from *You Can't Eat Your Chicken Pox, Amber Brown* by Paula Danziger.

Talk About It

1. What two details help you visualize Aunt Pam?

2. What are you visualizing about Amber? What details from the story and what from your experience help you visualize her?

First Day in London

by Paula Danziger

"Elevators Ho," I yell as we enter the elevator.

There are mirrors in it.

Aunt Pam looks really good. She's wearing a flowered sundress and carrying a really pretty sweater.

Her long blond hair is in one long braid.

And she has makeup on and this really pretty-smelling perfume.

On her feet are walking shoes.

Aunt Pam is ready to show me London.

I look in the mirror.

I'm wearing a long purple shirt. The shirt is so long that it's hard to see the denim shorts under it.

I've got sandals on.

My hair is just hanging there.

It was too tired to get put into ponytails or anything.

I'm not sure that I am ready for London.

As we leave the building, I hear someone call out, "Pam, welcome back."

Aunt Pam turns and smiles. "Amber, I want to introduce you to Mary. She's the housekeeper here . . . and over the years has become a friend."

"Welcome to London, Amber. Is this your first time in our city?"

I smile and nod. "It's Amber's first day and we're off to see Trafalgar Square," Aunt Pam tells Mary as she takes my hand and walks up to the curb to get a cab. Even though I'm too big to hold hands anymore, I hold her hand. "Amber, do you remember what I told you about cars in this country?"

I'm so tired . . . and the cars are driving on the wrong side of the road, just like Aunt Pam told me.

LOOK AHEAD

In "The Extra-Good Sunday," Ramona and Beezus have to cook Sunday dinner for the whole family. Read and visualize how they prepare the family meal.

Vocabulary

Words to Know

| flushed | pronounced | sauce |
| hurled | refrigerator | success |

Words with similar meanings are **synonyms.** You can figure out the meaning of an unknown word by looking for a clue around it. The clue might be a synonym.

Read the paragraph below. Notice how *threw* helps you understand what *hurled* means.

The Quick Cook!

Leah wanted to make a special ice-cream <u>sauce</u> for Grandma's party, but the party was in two hours! She took milk from the <u>refrigerator</u>. Then she <u>hurled</u> chocolate chips into a bowl—she just threw them in so she could be quick. "Finished—just in time," <u>pronounced</u> Leah. Her face was <u>flushed</u> and red from running around the kitchen, but the delicious sauce was a <u>success</u>.

Write About It

Write about the first time someone you know tried to cook something. Use several vocabulary words.

The Extra-Good Sunday

from *Ramona Quimby, Age 8*
by Beverly Cleary

Life is strange! Dad has to draw his foot for art class! Mom put a raw egg into Ramona's school lunch by mistake! Then Mom made beef tongue for dinner on Saturday, and Beezus and Ramona complained! Now, as punishment, the girls must make Sunday dinner.

Sunday morning Ramona and Beezus were still resolved to be perfect until dinner time. They got up without being called, avoided arguing over who should read Dear Abby's advice first in the paper, complimented their mother on her French toast, and went off through the drizzly rain to Sunday school neat, combed, and bravely smiling.

Later they cleaned up their rooms without being told. At lunchtime they ate without complaint the sandwiches they knew were made of ground-up tongue. A little added pickle relish did not fool them, but it did help. They dried the dishes and carefully avoided looking in the direction of the refrigerator lest their mother be reminded they were supposed to cook the evening meal.

Mr. and Mrs. Quimby were good-humored. In fact, everyone was so unnaturally pleasant that Ramona almost wished someone would say something cross. By early afternoon, the question was still hanging in the air. Would the girls really have to prepare dinner?

Why doesn't somebody say something? Ramona thought, weary of being so good, weary of longing to forgive her mother for the raw egg in her lunch.

"Well, back to the old foot," said Mr. Quimby, as he once more settled himself on the couch with drawing pad and pencil and pulled off his shoe and sock.

The rain finally stopped. Ramona watched for dry spots to appear on the sidewalk and thought of her roller skates in the closet. She looked into Beezus's room and found her sister reading. Ramona knew Beezus wanted to telephone Mary Jane but had decided to wait until Mary Jane called to ask why she had not come over. Mary Jane did not call. The day dragged on.

When dry spots on the concrete in front of the Quimbys' house widened until moisture remained only in the cracks of the sidewalk, Ramona pulled her skates out of her closet. To her father, who was holding a drawing of his foot at arm's length to study it, she said, "Well, I guess I'll go out and skate."

"Aren't you forgetting something?" he asked.

"What?" asked Ramona, knowing very well what.

"Dinner," he said.

The question that had hung in the air all day was answered. The matter was settled.

"We're stuck," Ramona told Beezus. "Now we can stop being so good."

The sisters went into the kitchen, shut the door, and opened the refrigerator.

"A package of chicken thighs," said Beezus with a groan. "And a package of frozen peas. And yogurt, one carton of plain and one of banana. There must have been a special on yogurt." She closed the refrigerator and reached for a cookbook.

"I could make place cards," said Ramona, as Beezus frantically flipped pages.

"We can't eat place cards," said Beezus. "Besides, corn bread is your job because you brought it up." Both girls spoke in whispers. There was no need to let their parents, their mean old parents, know what was going on in the kitchen.

In her mother's recipe file, Ramona found the card for corn bread written in Mr. Quimby's grandmother's shaky handwriting, which Ramona found difficult to read.

"I can't find a recipe for chicken thighs," said Beezus, "just whole chicken. All I know is that Mother bakes thighs in the flat glass dish with some kind of sauce."

"Mushroom soup mixed with something and with some kind of little specks stirred in." Ramona remembered that much from watching her mother.

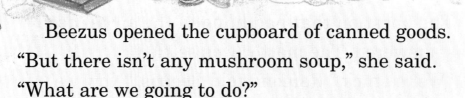

Beezus opened the cupboard of canned goods. "But there isn't any mushroom soup," she said. "What are we going to do?"

"Mix up something wet," suggested Ramona. "It would serve them right if it tasted awful."

"Why don't we make something awful?" asked Beezus. "So they will know how we feel when we have to eat tongue."

"What tastes really awful?" Ramona was eager to go along with the suggestion, united with her sister against their enemy—for the moment, their parents.

Beezus, always practical, changed her mind. "It wouldn't work. We have to eat it too, and they're so mean we'll probably have to do the dishes besides. Anyway, I guess you might say our honor is at stake, because they think we can't cook a good meal."

Ramona was ready with another solution. "Throw everything in one dish."

Beezus opened the package of chicken thighs and stared at them with distaste. "I can't stand touching raw meat," she said, as she picked up a thigh between two forks.

"Do we have to eat the skin?" asked Ramona. "All those yucky little bumps."

Beezus found a pair of kitchen tongs. She tried holding down a thigh with a fork and pulling off the skin with the tongs.

"Here, let me hold it," said Ramona, who was not squeamish about touching such things as worms or raw meat. She took a firm hold on the thigh while Beezus grasped the skin with the tongs. Both pulled, and the skin peeled away. They played tug-of-war with each thigh, leaving a sad-looking heap of skins on the counter and a layer of chicken thighs in the glass dish.

"Can't you remember what little specks Mother uses?" asked Beezus. Ramona could not. The girls studied the spice shelf, unscrewed jar lids and sniffed. Nutmeg? No. Cloves? Terrible. Cinnamon?

Uh-uh. Chili powder? Well . . . Yes, that must be it. Ramona remembered that the specks were red. Beezus stirred half a teaspoon of the dark red powder into the yogurt, which she poured over the chicken. She slid the dish into the oven set at 350 degrees, the temperature for chicken recommended by the cookbook.

From the living room came the sound of their parents' conversation, sometimes serious and sometimes highlighted by laughter. While we're slaving out here, thought Ramona, as she climbed up on the counter to reach the box of cornmeal. After she climbed down, she discovered she had to climb up again for baking powder and soda. She finally knelt on the counter to save time and asked Beezus to bring her an egg.

"It's a good thing Mother can't see you up there," remarked Beezus, as she handed Ramona an egg.

"How else am I supposed to reach things?" Ramona successfully broke the egg and tossed the shell onto the counter. "Now I need buttermilk."

Beezus broke the news. There was no buttermilk in the refrigerator. "What'll I do?" whispered Ramona in a panic.

"Here. Use this." Beezus thrust the carton of banana yogurt at her sister. "Yogurt is sort of sour, so it might work."

The kitchen door opened a crack. "What's going on in there?" inquired Mr. Quimby.

Beezus hurled herself against the door. "You stay out!" she ordered. "Dinner is going to be a—surprise!"

For a moment Ramona thought Beezus had been going to say a mess. She stirred egg and yogurt together, measured flour, spilling some on the floor, and then discovered she was short of cornmeal. More panic.

"My cooking teacher says you should always check to see if you have all the ingredients before you start to cook," said Beezus.

"Oh, be quiet." Ramona reached for a package of Cream of Wheat, because its grains were about the same size as cornmeal. She scattered only a little on the floor.

Something was needed to sop up the sauce with little red specks when the chicken was served. Rice! The spilled Cream of Wheat gritted underneath Beezus's feet as she measured rice and boiled water according to the directions on the package.

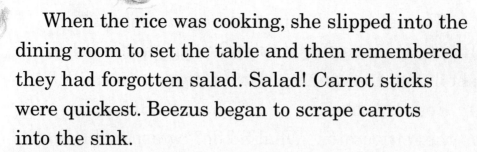

When the rice was cooking, she slipped into the dining room to set the table and then remembered they had forgotten salad. Salad! Carrot sticks were quickest. Beezus began to scrape carrots into the sink.

"Yipe!" yelped Ramona from the counter. "The rice!" The lid of the pan was chittering. Beezus snatched a larger pan from the cupboard and transferred the rice.

"Do you girls need any help?" Mrs. Quimby called from the living room.

"No!" answered her daughters.

Another calamity. The corn bread should bake at 400 degrees, a higher temperature than that needed for the chicken. What was Ramona to do?

"Stick it in the oven anyway." Beezus's face was flushed.

In went the corn bread beside the chicken.

"Dessert!" whispered Beezus. All she could find was a can of boring pear halves. Back to the cookbook. "Heat with a little butter and serve with jelly in each half," she read. Jelly. Half a jar of apricot jam would have to do. The pears and butter went into the saucepan. Never mind the syrup spilled on the floor.

"Beezus!" Ramona held up the package of peas.

Beezus groaned. Out came the partially cooked chicken while she stirred the thawing peas into the yogurt and shoved the dish back into the oven.

The rice! They had forgotten the rice, which was only beginning to stick to the pan. Quick! Take it off the burner. How did their mother manage to get everything cooked at the right time? Put the carrot sticks on a dish. Pour the milk. "Candles!" Beezus whispered. "Dinner might look better if we have candles."

Ramona found two candle holders and two partly melted candles of uneven length. One of them had been used in a Halloween jack-o'-lantern. Beezus struck the match to light them, because although Ramona was brave about touching raw meat, she was skittish about lighting matches.

Was the chicken done? The girls anxiously examined their main dish, bubbling and brown around the edges. Beezus stabbed a thigh with a fork, and when it did not bleed, she decided it must be done. A toothpick pricked into the corn bread came out clean. The corn bread was done— flat, but done.

Grit, grit, grit sounded under the girls' feet.
It was amazing how a tiny bit of spilled Cream of
Wheat could make the entire kitchen floor gritty.
At last their dinner was served, the dining-room
light turned off, dinner announced, and the cooks,
tense with anxiety that was hidden by candlelight,
fell into their chairs as their parents seated
themselves. Was this dinner going to be edible?

"Candles!" exclaimed Mrs. Quimby. "What a
festive meal!"

"Let's taste it before we decide," said Mr.
Quimby with his most wicked grin.

The girls watched anxiously as their father took his first bite of the chicken. He chewed thoughtfully and said with more surprise than necessary, "Why this is good!"

"It really is," agreed Mrs. Quimby, and took a bit of corn bread. "Very good, Ramona," she said.

Mr. Quimby tasted the corn bread. "Just like Grandmother used to make," he pronounced.

The girls exchanged suppressed smiles. They could not taste the banana yogurt, and by candlelight, no one could tell that the corn bread was a little pale. The chicken, Ramona decided, was not as good as her parents thought—or pretended to think—but she could eat it without gagging.

Everyone relaxed, and Mrs. Quimby said chili powder was more interesting than paprika and asked which recipe they had used for the chicken.

Ramona answered, "Our own," as she exchanged another look with Beezus. Paprika! Those little specks in the sauce should have been paprika.

"We wanted to be creative," said Beezus.

Conversation was more comfortable than it had been the previous evening. Mr. Quimby said he was finally satisfied with his drawing which looked like a real foot. Beezus said her cooking class was studying the food groups everyone should eat every day. Ramona said there was this boy at school who called her Egghead. Mr. Quimby explained that Egghead was slang for a very smart person.

Ramona began to feel better.

The meal was a success. If the chicken did not taste as good as the girls had hoped and the corn bread did not rise like their mother's, both were edible. Beezus and Ramona were silently grateful to their parents for enjoying—or pretending to enjoy—their cooking. The whole family cheered up. When they had finished their pears with apricot jam, Ramona gave her mother a shy smile.

Mrs. Quimby smiled back and patted Ramona's hand. Ramona felt much lighter. Without using words, she had forgiven her mother for the unfortunate egg, and her mother had understood. Ramona could be happy again.

"You cooks have worked so hard," said Mr. Quimby, "that I'm going to wash the dishes. I'll even finish clearing the table."

"I'll help," volunteered Mrs. Quimby.

The girls exchanged another secret smile as they excused themselves and skipped off to their rooms before their parents discovered the pile of chicken skins and the broken eggshell on the counter, the carrot scrapings in the sink, and the Cream of Wheat, flour, and pear syrup on the floor.

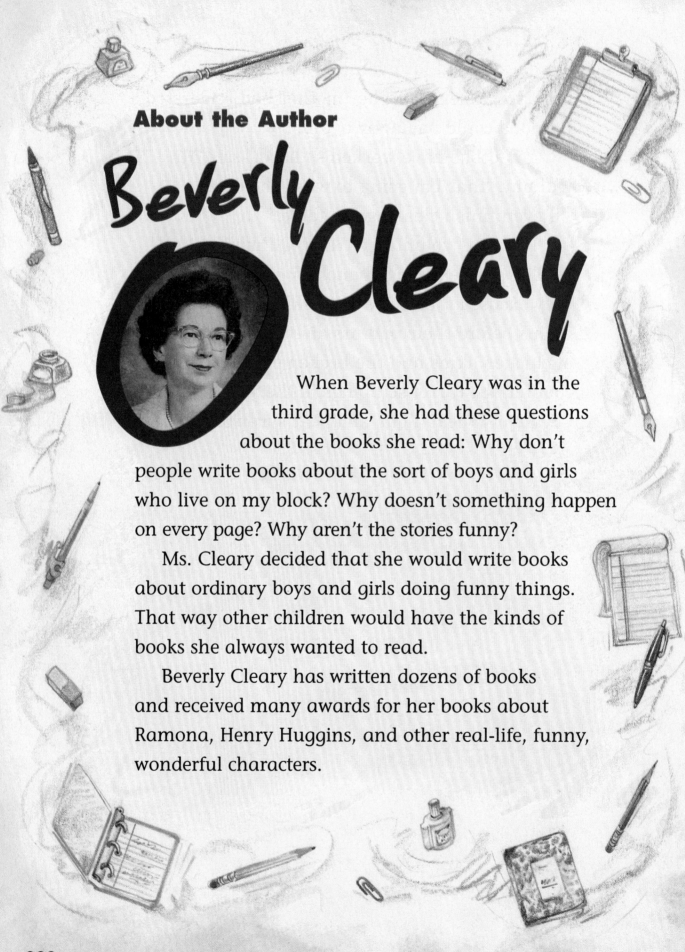

About the Author

Beverly Cleary

When Beverly Cleary was in the third grade, she had these questions about the books she read: Why don't people write books about the sort of boys and girls who live on my block? Why doesn't something happen on every page? Why aren't the stories funny?

Ms. Cleary decided that she would write books about ordinary boys and girls doing funny things. That way other children would have the kinds of books she always wanted to read.

Beverly Cleary has written dozens of books and received many awards for her books about Ramona, Henry Huggins, and other real-life, funny, wonderful characters.

Reader Response

Open for Discussion

Have you had a frantic but funny time over food as Beezus and Ramona do? Tell about it.

Comprehension Check

1. Are the Quimbys a happy family or an unhappy family? Support your answer with examples.

2. Do you think that Beezus and Ramona do a good job fixing dinner? Use details to support your answer.

3. What do you think Mom and Dad will say and do when they see the messy kitchen? Why do you think so?

4. Use all of your senses to **visualize** the dinner table when the Quimby family sits down to eat. What details from the story help you? (Visualizing)

5. Think about the mess in the kitchen. What senses can you use to **visualize** the scene? Describe the kitchen. (Visualizing)

 Test Prep

Look Back and Write

Look back at page 333. Beezus thinks Ramona is skittish about lighting matches. What does *skittish* mean? Use context clues to help you.

Test Prep

How to Read a Poem

1. Preview

- Look at the title of the poem. Do you think the poem will have realistic details or exaggerations? How can you tell?

2. Read and Listen

- Read the poem. How can you tell the speaker has really made pizza?

- Listen for phrases the speaker uses to exaggerate, or say that things are larger or greater than they really are. List your favorites. Why do you think the speaker exaggerates when he talks about making his pizza?

3. Think and Connect

Think about "The Extra-Good Sunday." Then look at your list of exaggerations from "A Pizza the Size of the Sun."

If the speaker were cooking in the kitchen with Beezus and Ramona, what would he say to them? What would Beezus and Ramona say to the speaker?

A Pizza the Size of the Sun

by Jack Prelutsky

I'm making a pizza the size of the sun,
a pizza that's sure to weigh more than a ton,
a pizza too massive to pick up and toss,
a pizza resplendent with oceans of sauce.

I'm topping my pizza with mountains of cheese,
with acres of peppers, pimentos, and peas,
with mushrooms, tomatoes, and sausage galore,
with every last olive they had at the store.

My pizza is sure to be one of a kind,
my pizza will leave other pizzas behind,
my pizza will be a delectable treat
that all who love pizza are welcome to eat.

The oven is hot, I believe it will take
a year and a half for my pizza to bake—
I hardly can wait till my pizza is done,
my wonderful pizza the size of the sun.

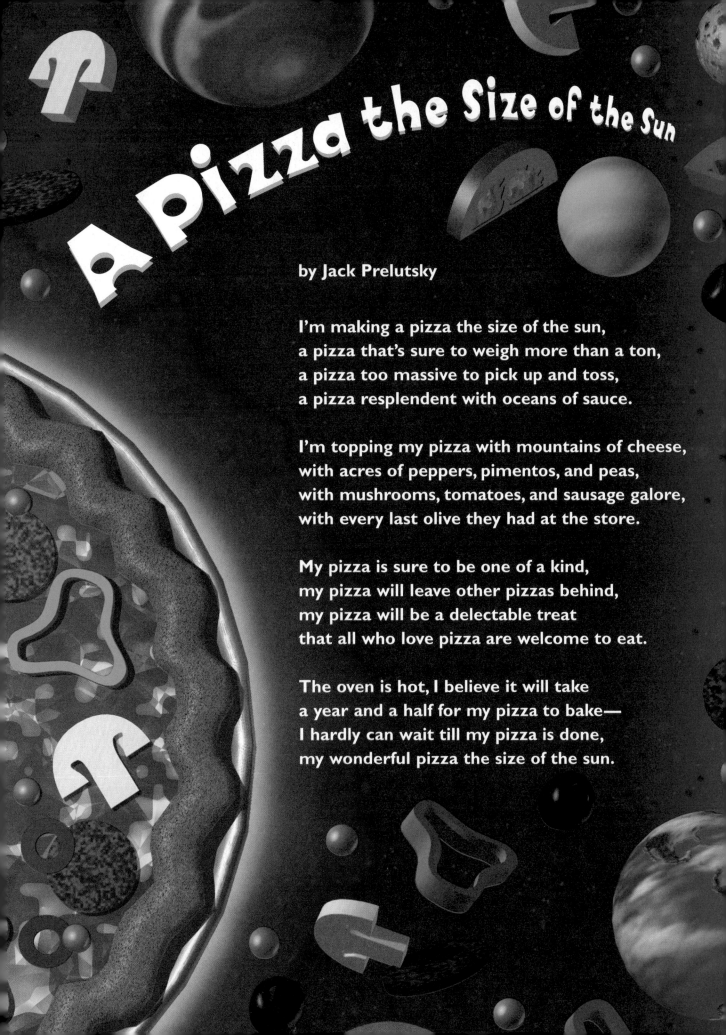

Plot

- **Plot** includes the important events of a story that happen in the beginning, middle, and end and how those events happen.

- Events that are important to the plot help keep the story going.

Read "A Moon Landing" from _Grandpa Takes Me to the Moon_ by Timothy R. Gaffney.

Write About It

1. Look at the beginning of the story. Write two important events that happen in the beginning.

2. Write two important events that happen in the middle of the story. Share them with a classmate.

A Moon Landing
by Timothy R. Gaffney

A boy imagines himself landing on the moon with his grandfather, who had been an astronaut.

We touch down on a flat plain with round, gray mountains on the horizon. There are no colors, just shades of gray. The sun is shining, but the sky is black like night. There is no air on the moon to make the sky blue. Space and black sky come right down to the ground.

We put on our space helmets. We have to back out the little door on our hands and knees. We climb down the ladder and step onto the moon.

Our spacesuits are thick and heavy, but everything weighs much less on the moon. Grandpa bounces when he walks. I pick up a rock and let it drop. It falls in slow motion to the ground.

Dust splashes up around it and falls back like water.

We unload the buggy. Grandpa calls it the lunar rover. We drive away on it until the moon lander looks like a little toy.

We stop several times to scoop up soil and rocks to take back to Earth. Pieces of the moon. We scoop them up and put them in bags, just like that.

High overhead is the Earth. It reminds me of the moon when it's almost full, but its bright side is colored blue and white by oceans and clouds.

"Time to go home," Grandpa says.

Before we leave, we plant an American flag on the moon. A small arm on the flagpole holds the flag out like it's waving in a breeze. We step back and salute it. Then we climb back into the moon lander and blast off.

We return to the capsule and it takes us back to earth. Splash! We're home.

LOOK AHEAD

In *Floating Home*, a girl decides to draw her house from space. Read and discover how the plot's important events happen as she makes her way into space.

Vocabulary

Words to Know

**astronaut   launch   weighed
emergency   unusual   globe**

Words with opposite meanings are
antonyms. You can often figure out
the meaning of an unknown word by
finding a clue nearby. Sometimes this
clue is an antonym.

Read the paragraph below. Notice
how *ordinary* helps you understand
the meaning of *unusual*.

A Letter Home from Space Camp

Being here has been so <u>unusual</u>—not like an
ordinary summer at home! We learned how an
<u>astronaut</u> circles the <u>globe</u> in a spaceship. We
saw a film of a shuttle <u>launch</u> and learned how
pilots make <u>emergency</u> landings if things go
wrong. Our group went on a "moon mission."
I <u>weighed</u> a lot less on the moon than on Earth!
I'll tell you more when I'm home.

Write About It

Write a headline about the latest
mission in space—real or imaginary.
Use some vocabulary words.

Floating Home

written by David Getz
illustrated by Michael Rex

When Mrs. Selinsky asked the class to look at their homes in a new way and to draw what they saw, Maxine left school and kept on walking.

She passed Kevin outside his house, sitting on the branch of a tree, studying his home as if he were a squirrel.

She passed Selina lying in the grass in her front yard, looking up at her apartment building as if she were an ant.

She passed Oscar in dark sunglasses, standing in front of his home, pretending he was a stranger.

Artist's pad under her arm, her unsharpened colored pencils in their box, and a globe sharpener with all the countries of the world in her overalls pocket, Maxine passed her own home and kept on walking.

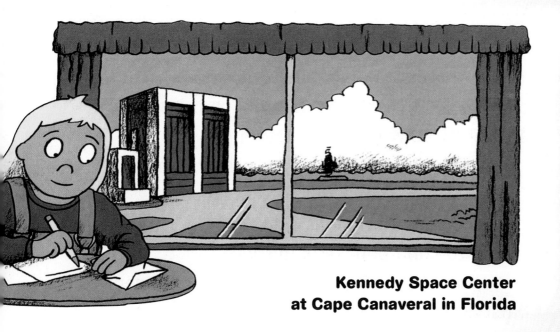

**Kennedy Space Center
at Cape Canaveral in Florida**

She was going to draw the most unusual picture of all, a picture of the Earth from space. She was going to be the youngest astronaut of all time!

Maxine checked into her room, wrote a letter to her mom and dad, and undressed to take a shower.

She knew it would be the last shower she would take for two weeks.

You don't shower in the space shuttle. Water does not fall from the nozzle.

Nothing falls inside a shuttle in space. Water spraying out of a shower would float all over the place and quickly fill the cabin with dancing beads of liquid.

Maxine turned on the hot water. She let herself disappear in a cloud of steam.

She washed her hair.

She opened a window to let the steam escape.

Her last breakfast on Earth was in three hours.

Her crewmates ate very little.

Maxine had a cup of orange juice and a bowl of cereal.

She was disappointed there was no prize in her cereal box. She watched the milk pour from the container. Down it flowed. Down.

Soon there would be no down in the shuttle. Down is where things fall.

In space, nothing falls.

She couldn't pour milk in space.

Suddenly newspaper and television reporters burst into the room.

"Maxine!" one of them called out. "Are you afraid?"

"Maxine," another asked, "how does it feel to be the first eight-year-old astronaut?"

"Maxine, are you going to miss your parents?"

"Maxine, why are you doing it?"

"Art," Maxine told them. "I'm doing it for art."

"Time to get dressed!" said a NASA official.

More reporters were waiting for her in the suit room. They were there to watch her get dressed.

She was glad this didn't happen at home every morning.

The pressure suit was meant to protect her should anything happen to the shuttle before it rose to nineteen miles above the ground. The suit was big and orange, and she didn't put it on as much as climb into it. Through a slit in the back Maxine shoved one leg, then the other, and then her arms. She poked her head through the tight neck band at the top of the suit. The boots locked onto the pants cuffs. The gloves locked onto the sleeves, and the helmet locked onto the collar.

The people from NASA put all sorts of things in her pockets: special gloves to keep her warm if she needed to parachute out of the shuttle and land in the ocean; an emergency radio; survival gear; sharpener and colored pencils. They also gave her a small mirror.

"Place it on your lap," someone said. "You'll be able to see out the window above your head."

It was time to go out to the pad.

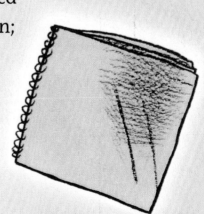

Feeling like a hundred-pound duck, Maxine waddled over to the van that would take her to the launch pad.

It was 3 A.M. and dark outside. Maxine had never been outside at 3 A.M. before.

"So this is what the world looks like when I'm sleeping," she said to herself.

And then she saw the shuttle.

It was alive.

Suspended above the pad, the vehicle was lit by dazzlingly bright xenon lights as if it were an actor, stage center, ready for his big speech.

And it was breathing. Exhaling steam from its top and bottom, it reminded Maxine of a dragon.

The orbiter itself looked like a stubby airplane. It rode piggyback on a huge orange fuel tank as tall as a fifteen-story building. Filled with liquid hydrogen and oxygen, the orange tank would supply the fuel for the shuttle's main engines.

On either side of the orange tank were the two solid rocket boosters. Loaded with chunks of solid fuel like skyscrapers stuffed with gunpowder, these boosters would help lift the shuttle off the pad and into space.

Maxine entered the shuttle's orbiter through a porthole. Since the shuttle was pointed straight up, ready for launch, the back wall was actually her floor. To protect the panels and instruments from the astronauts' heavy feet, the wall was covered with a thick pad.

"Some art project," a technician said, and helped strap Maxine into her seat.

"I hope your mom puts your drawing on her refrigerator," another technician said, and checked her suit. He made sure it was in working order.

The technicians removed the padding covering the back wall and, one by one, stepped out through the porthole.

As the door closed, Maxine checked to make sure her pad, pencils, and sharpener were still there.

The countdown began.

With two minutes to go, the controllers at Cape Canaveral announced over the radio, "Close and lock your visors. Turn on your suit oxygen. Have a nice flight."

Maxine placed the mirror on her lap. She could see through the window above her head. She saw nothing but clouds and a clear blue sky.

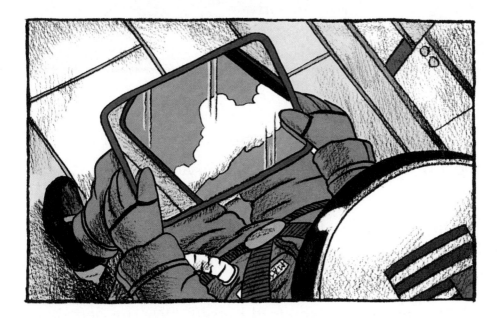

Then she did as she was told. She lowered her visor and began to breathe oxygen from her suit.

The main engines started. Everything began to tremble. It was a familiar feeling, like being in a subway train. The vibrations jostled her mirror.

Then the whole shuttle began to sway.

Suddenly the rumbling became thunderous; the gentle subway became an earthquake. Everything shuddered and shook.

The shuttle swayed back. The solid rockets ignited.

The noise!

Like a thousand thousand lions roaring! Like the heart of an immense raging fire. *Roar!*

Boom!

She was pressed deep into her seat.

Then something kicked her in the back.

Then . . . up!

"We are going!" she told herself. "We are definitely going somewhere!"

Up! Up!

Launch!

Looking into her mirror, she could see the launch pad dropping away at a dizzying speed. Rapidly everything on the ground became smaller and smaller.

Up! Up!

One . . . two . . . three . . . four . . . five . . . six . . . seven . . . flying faster and faster . . . eight! The shuttle began to roll.

Over, then over.

Maxine watched the sunlight fly across the cabin.

She was flying upside down.

Invisible hands pushed her deep into her seat.

The shuttle hurtled through the thick atmosphere.

The wind howled.

In twenty seconds, she was traveling faster than the speed of sound, faster than the word *hello* travels from one person's mouth to another's ear—760 miles per hour! One mile every five seconds!

Faster, then faster. The shuttle tore through the thick atmosphere.

At two minutes, their fuel completely used up, the solid rocket boosters were no longer necessary. It was time to get rid of them.

Bang! The separation motors jettisoned the solid rocket boosters away from the shuttle. It felt like a giant had whacked the shuttle with a big stick.

The cabin lit up. For a frightening second everything was fire and smoke outside the windows.

Then clear.

Then quiet.

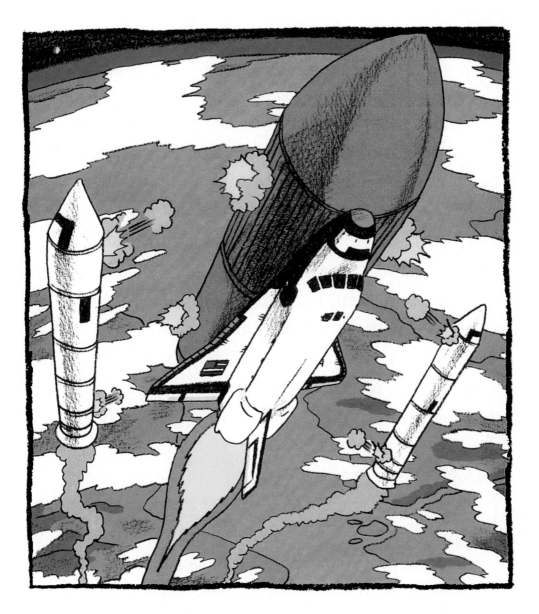

Maxine imagined the empty rocket canisters under their parachutes, drifting back down to Earth. They would be picked up in the ocean.

Now the ride was glass smooth. And impossibly fast.

Within eight minutes of launch, Maxine was traveling 11,000 miles per hour, or almost 190 miles a minute. Three miles a second.

The acceleration continued to press her deep into her seat, made her face feel as if a heavy weight were pushing against it, made her chest feel as if a gorilla were sitting on her ribs.

It was hard to breathe. She took quick, shallow, sharp breaths.

She couldn't move, couldn't lift her arms.

Then the three main engines cut off.

Suddenly everything was funny. In less than a heartbeat, Maxine went from feeling as if she weighed two hundred pounds to feeling as if she weighed nothing at all.

She was in space.

Her eyes seemed to float in her head. Her stomach floated in her belly. She floated within her suit.

She felt giddy . . . and a little sick.

"We made it!"

Someone laughed.

All around the cabin, things were floating. Checklists attached to panels by strings drifted like sea plants. Her mirror gently tumbled over and over through the air of the cabin.

"Maxine," someone called to her, "look up!"
There in the window was Earth.

It was dazzling, sitting like a royal-blue gem on black velvet.

At its curved edge, on the horizon, was a thin, bright, fluorescent-blue band. The atmosphere.

She was looking down at the air she had breathed.

Somewhere down there her house sat at the bottom of the atmosphere. Her parents were breathing its air.

Suddenly something drew a long, thin streak beneath her.

It was a shooting star. A chunk of rock from space had sliced through the atmosphere and burned up.

She was looking down at the shooting stars.

The shuttle passed over a funnel of clouds, a hurricane. Where the sky was clear, she could see shades of brown, gray, green. All that blue.

But where was her home? Where was her town, her city? Her state? She removed her globe sharpener, with all the countries.

She looked out the window. Somebody had forgotten to draw in the lines! Where were the lines that divided up the continents into countries? Where were the lines that divided up the countries into states, the states into cities?

There were no lines. It was just one Earth.

It was her home.

About the Author
David Getz

Is *Floating Home* a science book or isn't it? In this story, David Getz combines fiction and nonfiction to create a story about a girl who goes into space. Mr. Getz wrote the book *Floating Home* after interviewing astronauts and officials from the National Aeronautics and Space Administration (NASA).

Mr. Getz is an elementary school science teacher in New York City. He and his wife have one daughter, Maxine.

About the Illustrator
Michael Rex

Michael Rex says that "being an astronaut is the only profession I'd give up drawing for." *Floating Home* is the first book that Mr. Rex illustrated. Since then, he has illustrated other books, including *The Painting Gorilla*, which he also wrote. Michael Rex lives in New York.

Reader Response

Open for Discussion

If you had a chance to go on the space shuttle with Maxine, would you go? What would your home look like from space?

Comprehension Check

1. What did Mrs. Selinsky mean when she told students to look at their homes in a new way? Do you think she expected students to do what Maxine did?

2. What kind of person is Maxine? What parts of the story support your ideas?

3. Could this story really happen? Use details to support your answer.

4. List three main **plot** events in *Floating Home*. (Plot)

5. Is Maxine writing a letter home an important **plot** event? (Plot)

Test Prep

Look Back and Write

Look back at pages 353–361. What happened after the shuttle took off? Use the text and pictures to tell the main events in order.

Chris

Spacewalk Talk
Interview with astronaut Chris Hadfield

by Peter Wanyenya with Keltie Thomas

Peter

Peter: What was your first space mission like? Were you nervous?

Chris: My first space mission, which is the only one I've gone on so far, was to go build the Russian space station Mir. It really wasn't too scary—mostly because we had trained so much.

What's your favorite thing about space?
Weightlessness—to be floating free.

Why is that so neat?
Well, people like trampolines, swing sets, scuba diving, and skydiving. They do all those things because they like feeling that little bit of weightlessness.

So imagine how much fun it is when you're on a spaceship and weightlessness is permanent. It's like you're skydiving forever.

What will you do on your mission later this year?
I'm doing spacewalks on STS-100. That's my primary job on that flight. I'll be the first Canadian to ever walk in space. I'll go outside the shuttle probably three times.

What will you do on your spacewalks?
The purpose of our flight is to take up the big Canadian space station arm. The big arm (that is, the one that's on the shuttle already) will pick it up and stick it onto the station like a big folded-up spider. So we're going to take a

The Lowdown on Chris's Mission

Mission number: STS-100

(STS stands for "Space Transport System," which includes the shuttle and all of its equipment.)

spacewalk and, by hand, unfold the arm and bolt it together. Then we'll plug in all of its wires and bring it to life.

So you'll be walking on the outside of the space station?

Well, you don't walk. The term "spacewalk" isn't really accurate. It's more like "spacefloat." So you always have to hold on to the shuttle or the station. But if you're trying to do something with two hands, that's really inefficient. So we have foot restraints. Once your feet are locked, you can work with your hands. And you wear a big "bat" utility belt (like Batman) with all of your tools on it.

What would happen if your feet popped out of the restraints?

We stay tethered, or roped in. But if you're doing a spacewalk outside the shuttle and you pop free or your tether breaks, the shuttle can fire its thrusters and come and get you.

How long do you spacewalk for?

About eight hours.

What do you do if you get hungry during a spacewalk?

They tried putting a little fruit roll-up in the helmet. So you could grab it with your teeth and chew it part way through the spacewalk. But the trouble was that it got crooked or you got a little water on it and it got all gooey. Then you had this big, gooey mess in there with your face. So they stopped doing that. Now we just eat before we go out!

Wow! It sounds like spacewalking can be a tough job! Which do you like better— working in mission control when you're not on a space mission or being up in space?

Working in mission control is the second best job that an astronaut can have. But working in space is the best thing!

Target launch date: November 30, 2000

Shuttle: Endeavour

Days in space: 11

Mission: To bring up and install a Canadian robot arm on the International Space Station

Spacewalks required during mission: 2 to 3

Realism and Fantasy

- A **realistic story** tells about something that could happen in real life.

- A **fantasy** has some things that could not possibly happen. Some also have things that could happen.

Read "Ali and the Snake" from *The Girl Who Wore Snakes* by Angela Johnson and "Verdi Wonders" from *Verdi* by Janell Cannon.

The Girl Who Wore Snakes
story by Angela Johnson · paintings by James E. Ransome

Write About It

1. Write *Snakes* at the top of a piece of paper. Write *realistic* at the top left and *fantasy* at the top right. Write details from each story under the correct word.

2. Decide which story is realistic and which one is a fantasy. Tell why you think as you do.

Ali and *the* Snake

by Angela Johnson

When the man from the zoo came to Ali's school, he brought Silvia, the snake.

She was brown, yellow, and orange, and made Ali think of the sun and the earth and everything in between.

The zoo man said, "Who wants to hold her?"

Ali said, "Me"—and wore Silvia, the brown, yellow, and orange snake, all day long around her neck, around her arms, and around her ankles.

After Silvia went back to the zoo, Ali became known as "the girl who wore the snake."

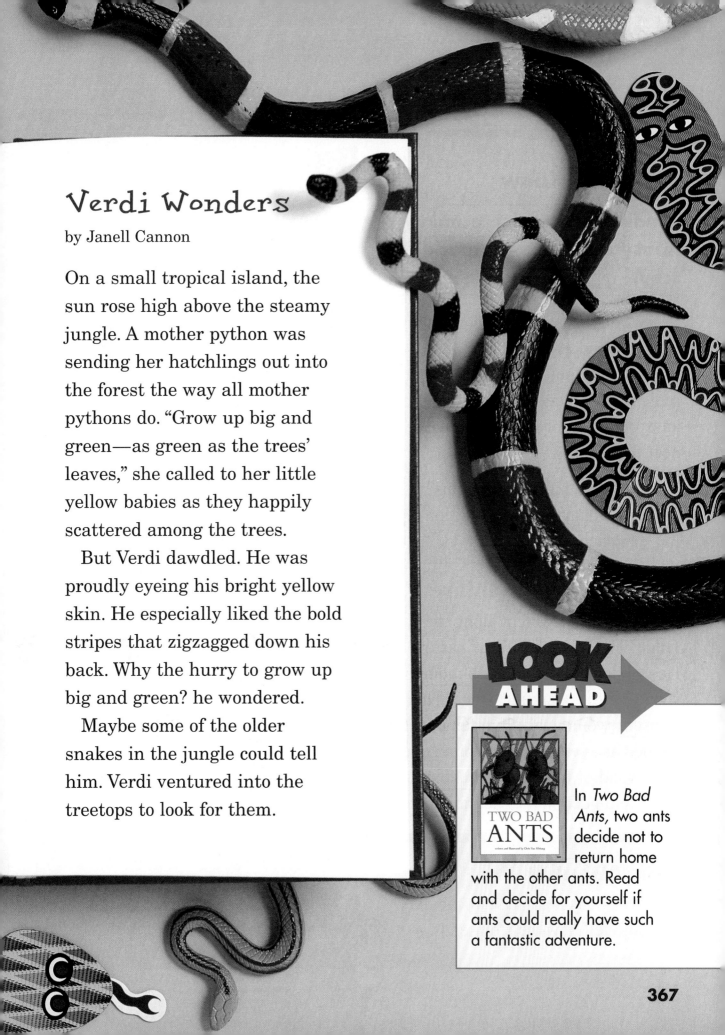

Verdi Wonders

by Janell Cannon

On a small tropical island, the sun rose high above the steamy jungle. A mother python was sending her hatchlings out into the forest the way all mother pythons do. "Grow up big and green—as green as the trees' leaves," she called to her little yellow babies as they happily scattered among the trees.

But Verdi dawdled. He was proudly eyeing his bright yellow skin. He especially liked the bold stripes that zigzagged down his back. Why the hurry to grow up big and green? he wondered.

Maybe some of the older snakes in the jungle could tell him. Verdi ventured into the treetops to look for them.

LOOK AHEAD

TWO BAD ANTS

In *Two Bad Ants*, two ants decide not to return home with the other ants. Read and decide for yourself if ants could really have such a fantastic adventure.

Vocabulary

Words to Know

blinding	crystal	echoing
treasure	ledge	sparkling
scout	remarkable	

When you read, you may come across a word you don't know. To figure out its meaning, look for clues in the other sentences. A clue might be found in an explanation or definition given near the word.

What do you think *ledge* means? Find an explanation or definition in a sentence near it.

A Dangerous Adventure

The scout slowly crept along the canyon's ledge. The rocky shelf was narrow and steep. He gripped the crystal as blinding sunlight shone off the sparkling stone. This remarkable treasure would make him famous. Suddenly he slipped and sent rocks tumbling over the side. The sound of falling rock echoing off the walls reminded him to be more careful.

Talk About It

What happens next? Use vocabulary words to tell how the story ends.

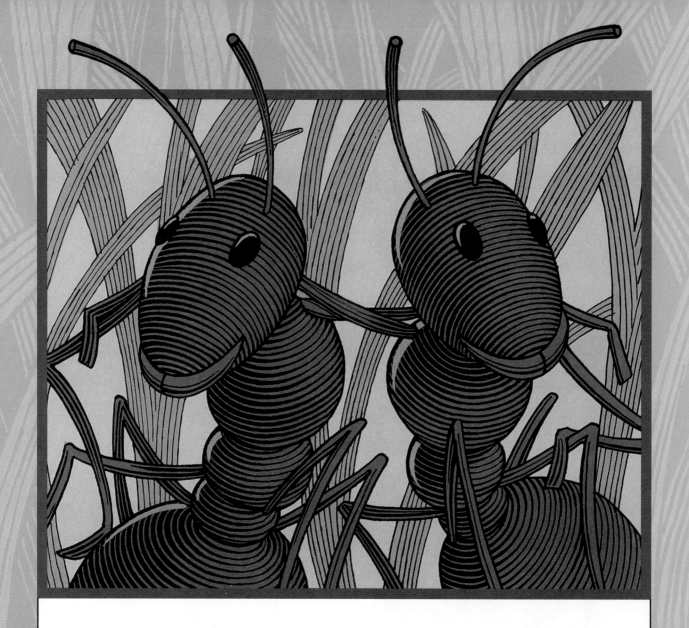

TWO BAD
ANTS

written and illustrated by Chris Van Allsburg

The news traveled swiftly through the tunnels of the ant world. A scout had returned with a remarkable discovery—a beautiful sparkling crystal. When the scout presented the crystal to the ant queen she took a small bite, then quickly ate the entire thing.

She deemed it the most delicious food she had ever tasted. Nothing could make her happier than to have more, much more. The ants understood. They were eager to gather more crystals because the queen was the mother of them all. Her happiness made the whole ant nest a happy place.

It was late in the day when they departed. Long shadows stretched over the entrance to the ant kingdom. One by one the insects climbed out, following the scout, who had made it clear—there were many crystals where the first had been found, but the journey was long and dangerous.

They marched into the woods that surrounded their underground home. Dusk turned to twilight, twilight to night. The path they followed twisted and turned, every bend leading them deeper into the dark forest.

More than once the line of ants stopped and anxiously listened for the sounds of hungry spiders. But all they heard was the call of the crickets echoing through the woods like distant thunder.

Dew formed on the leaves above. Without warning, huge cold drops fell on the marching ants. A firefly passed overhead that, for an instant, lit up the woods with a blinding flash of blue-green light.

At the edge of the forest stood a mountain. The ants looked up and could not see its peak. It seemed to reach right to the heavens. But they did not stop. Up the side they climbed, higher and higher.

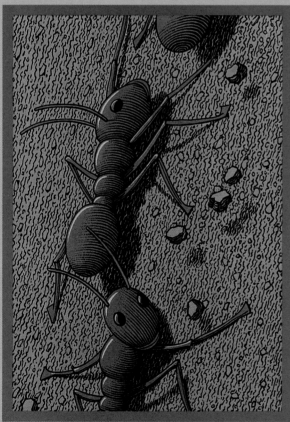

The wind whistled through the cracks of the mountain's face. The ants could feel its force bending their delicate antennae. Their legs grew weak as they struggled upward. At last they reached a ledge and crawled through a narrow tunnel.

When the ants came out of the tunnel they found themselves in a strange world. Smells they had known all their lives, smells of dirt and grass and rotting plants, had vanished. There was no more wind and, most puzzling of all, it seemed that the sky was gone.

They crossed smooth shiny surfaces, then followed the scout up a glassy, curved wall. They had reached their goal. From the top of the wall they looked below to a sea of crystals. One by one the ants climbed down into the sparkling treasure.

Quickly they each chose a crystal, then turned to start the journey home. There was something about this unnatural place that made the ants nervous. In fact they left in such a hurry that none of them noticed the two small ants who stayed behind.

"Why go back?" one asked the other. "This place may not feel like home, but look at all these crystals."

"You're right," said the other, "we can stay here and eat this tasty treasure every day, forever."

So the two ants ate crystal after crystal until they were too full to move, and fell asleep.

Daylight came. The sleeping ants were unaware of changes taking place in their new found home. A giant silver scoop hovered above them, then plunged deep into the crystals. It shoveled up both ants and crystals and carried them high into the air.

The ants were wide awake when the scoop turned, dropping them from a frightening height. They tumbled through space in a shower of crystals and fell into a boiling brown lake.

Then the giant scoop stirred violently back and forth. Crushing waves fell over the ants. They paddled hard to keep their tiny heads above water. But the scoop kept spinning the hot brown liquid.

Around and around it went, creating a whirlpool that sucked the ants deeper and deeper. They both held their breath and finally bobbed to the surface, gasping for air and spitting mouthfuls of the terrible, bitter water.

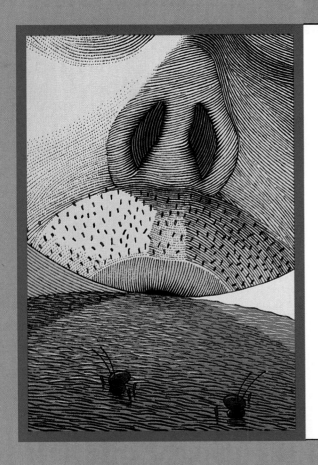

Then the lake tilted and began to empty into a cave. The ants could hear the rushing water and felt themselves pulled toward the pitch black hole.

Suddenly the cave disappeared and the lake became calm. The ants swam to the shore and found that the lake had steep sides.

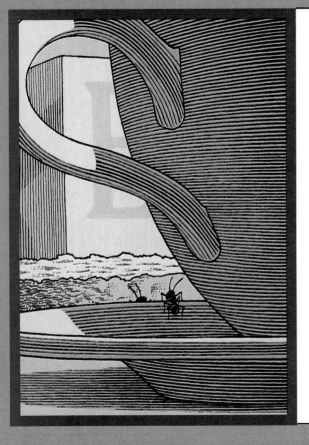

They hurried down the walls that held back the lake. The frightened insects looked for a place to hide, worried that the giant scoop might shovel them up again. Close by they found a huge round disk with holes that could neatly hide them.

But as soon as they had climbed inside, their hiding place was lifted, tilted, and lowered into a dark space. When the ants climbed out of the holes they were surrounded by a strange red glow. It seemed to them that every second the temperature was rising.

It soon became so unbearably hot that they thought they would soon be cooked. But suddenly the disk they were standing on rocketed upward and the two hot ants went flying through the air.

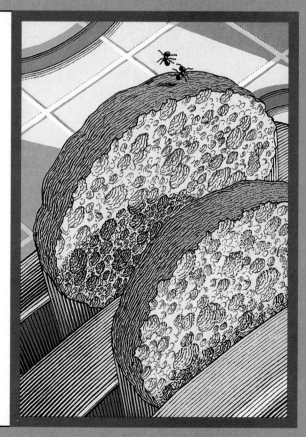

They landed near what seemed to be a fountain—a waterfall pouring from a silver tube. Both ants had a powerful thirst and longed to dip their feverish heads into the refreshing water. They quickly climbed along the tube.

As they got closer to the rushing water the ants felt a cool spray. They tightly gripped the shiny surface of the fountain and slowly leaned their heads into the falling stream. But the force of the water was much too strong.

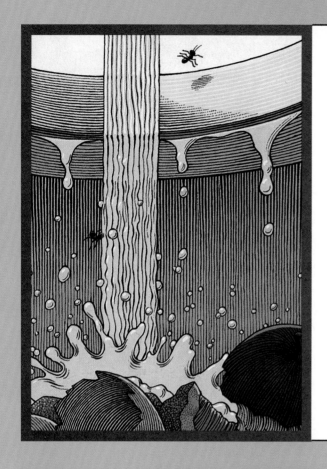

The tiny insects were pulled off the fountain and plunged down into a wet, dark chamber. They landed on half-eaten fruit and other soggy things. Suddenly the air was filled with loud, frightening sounds. The chamber began to spin.

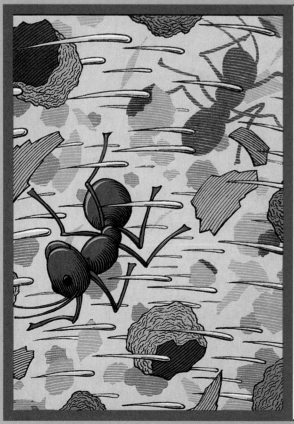

The ants were caught in a whirling storm of shredded food and stinging rain. Then, just as quickly as it had started, the noise and spinning stopped. Bruised and dizzy, the ants climbed out of the chamber.

In daylight once again, they raced through puddles and up a smooth metal wall. In the distance they saw something comforting—two long, narrow holes that reminded them of the warmth and safety of their old underground home. They climbed up into the dark openings.

But there was no safety inside these holes. A strange force passed through the wet ants. They were stunned senseless and blown out of the holes like bullets from a gun. When they landed the tiny insects were too exhausted to go on. They crawled into a dark corner and fell fast asleep.

Night had returned when the battered ants awoke to a familiar sound—the footsteps of their fellow insects returning for more crystals. The two ants slipped quietly to the end of the line. They climbed the glassy wall and once again stood amid the treasure. But this time they each chose a single crystal and followed their friends home.

Standing at the edge of their ant hole, the two ants listened to the joyful sounds that came from below. They knew how grateful their mother queen would be when they gave her their crystals. At that moment, the two ants felt happier than they'd ever felt before. This was their home, this was their family. This was where they were meant to be.

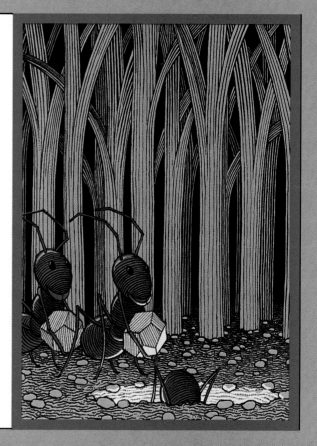

CHRIS VAN ALLSBURG

Chris Van Allsburg has been asked many times where his ideas come from. "The fact is," he says, "I don't know where my ideas come from. . . . It almost seems like a discovery, as if the story was always there. The few elements I start out with are actually clues. If I figure out what they mean, I can discover the story that's waiting."

When he creates a book, Mr. Van Allsburg usually begins by writing the story. He then makes rough sketches to decide from what angle each picture will be seen. When that is decided, he can experiment with light and shadows in his illustrations.

Mr. Van Allsburg likes to take walks and go to museums. He and his wife live in Rhode Island.

Reader Response

Open for Discussion

You are one of the bad ants. What will you tell your friends when you see them? Will you ever want to go exploring again? Why or why not?

Comprehension Check

1. Why do the two ants stay behind when the other ants take crystals to the queen? Use details to support your answer.

2. What word besides *bad* describes the ants? Use your word to write a new title. Support your title choice with examples from the story.

3. Look back at the story. What ordinary kitchen items become dangers to the ants?

4. *Two Bad Ants* is a **fantasy** because some things that happen in the story could not really happen. Name something from the story that could not really happen. (Realism and Fantasy)

5. Some things in a **fantasy** are real. Name two things from the story that could happen. (Realism and Fantasy)

 Test Prep

Look Back and Write

Was the author trying to entertain you, to persuade you, to inform you, or to describe or express something to you? Support your answer with details from the story.

PANDORA'S BOX

retold and illustrated by Anne Rockwell

Pandora was made, not born as other people are. Hephaestus modeled her out of clay. He made her a young woman as beautiful as his wife, Aphrodite, the goddess of love and beauty.

Each of the gods and goddesses gave Pandora a gift. Then Athene, the goddess of wisdom, breathed life into her. Most of the gifts the gods gave her were good ones. But unfortunately Hermes, as always full of tricks and mischief, gave her more curiosity than was good for her.

Pandora was sent to live on Earth. She had no trouble finding a good husband, for the gods and goddesses had given her the gifts of smiles and sweetness and wit and winning ways. Besides that, she was rich, for as a wedding gift the gods and goddesses gave her a box that had been made by Hephaestus. It was as beautiful as Pandora and very valuable too.

"Never, never open that box!" all the gods and goddesses warned Pandora. She promised to obey them, but as time went on Pandora grew more and more curious about what was in the box that she had promised never to open.

In those days, there was no sadness among the mortals on Earth. And why should it have been otherwise? There was no sickness, no hunger, no jealousy, no laziness, no greed, no anger, no cruelty. Even death was like a long and gentle sleep when people were very tired. There was no suffering of any kind.

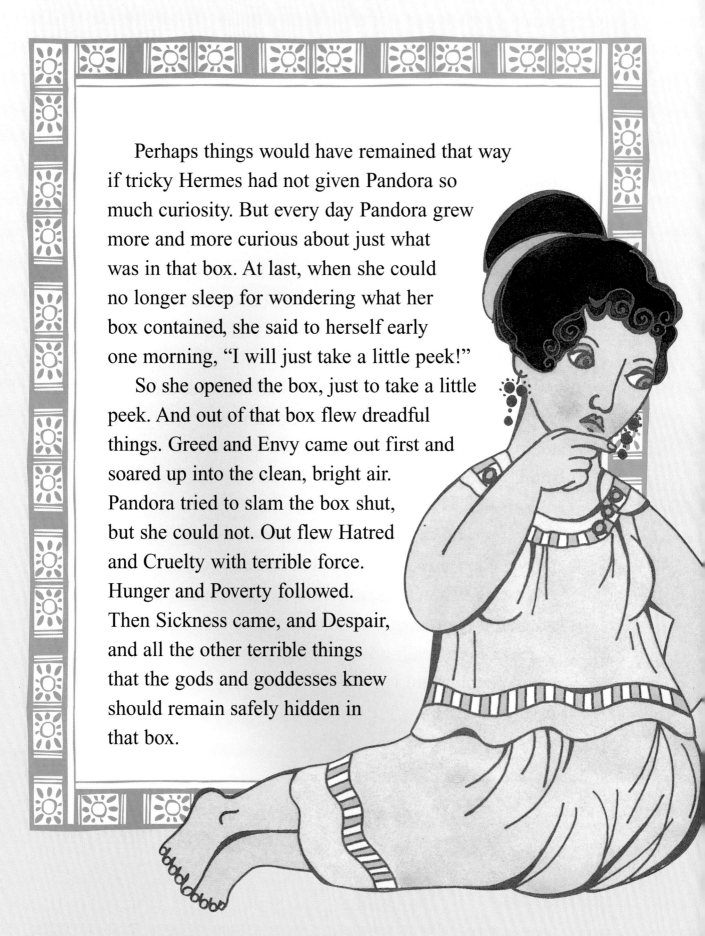

Perhaps things would have remained that way if tricky Hermes had not given Pandora so much curiosity. But every day Pandora grew more and more curious about just what was in that box. At last, when she could no longer sleep for wondering what her box contained, she said to herself early one morning, "I will just take a little peek!"

So she opened the box, just to take a little peek. And out of that box flew dreadful things. Greed and Envy came out first and soared up into the clean, bright air. Pandora tried to slam the box shut, but she could not. Out flew Hatred and Cruelty with terrible force. Hunger and Poverty followed. Then Sickness came, and Despair, and all the other terrible things that the gods and goddesses knew should remain safely hidden in that box.

Pandora had set them all free.

"Come back! Come back where you belong!" Pandora called out to the terrible things as they flew around her. She grabbed at them in the air, but they soared out of her reach and up into the sky. None came back. They are still out there bringing misery and trouble to people on Earth.

But the gods and goddesses had not put only dreadful things in Pandora's box. Hidden in among the terrible things was something small and fragile-winged and good. This thing was Hope. Who was the kindly god or goddess who thought to put Hope in among all the miseries and misfortunes? No one knows.

But because Hope was hidden in Pandora's box, whenever there is too much trouble and sadness among us mortals, Hope makes us think that tomorrow will be better.

And soon Pandora dried her tears.

"I hope I will never be too curious again!" she said.

And she never was.

Poetry

The Limerick's Lively to Write

by David McCord

The limerick's lively to write:
Five lines to it—all nice and tight.
　　Two long ones, two trick
　　Little short ones, then quick
As a flash here's the last one in sight.

There Was an Old Man with a Flute

by Edward Lear

There was an Old Man with a flute.
A serpent ran into his boot;
　　But he played day and night
　　'Til the serpent took flight,
And avoided that man with a flute.

I Love the Look of Words

by Maya Angelou

Popcorn leaps, popping from the floor
of a hot black skillet
and into my mouth.
Black words leap,
snapping from the white
page. Rushing into my eyes. Sliding
into my brain which gobbles them
the way my tongue and teeth
chomp the buttered popcorn.

When I have stopped reading,
ideas from the words stay stuck
in my mind, like the sweet
smell of butter perfuming my
fingers long after the popcorn
is finished.

I love the book and the look of words
the weight of ideas that popped into my mind
I love the tracks
of new thinking in my mind.

Hugs and Kisses

by Charlotte Pomerantz

Mami, how long will you be away?

I'll be gone for a month, María.

Then give me a kiss for every day,
For every day that you are away.

That's thirty small kisses, María.
Treinta besitos, one for each day.
One for each day that I am away.
Treinta besitos, María.

Now give me a hug for every day,
For every day that you are away.

That's thirty big hugs, María.
Treinta abrazos, one for each day.
One for each day that I am away.
Treinta abrazos, María.

Now give me a doll for every day,
For every day that you are away.

That's thirty dollies, María.
Treinta muñecas, one for each day.
One for each day that I am away.
No, indeed, María.

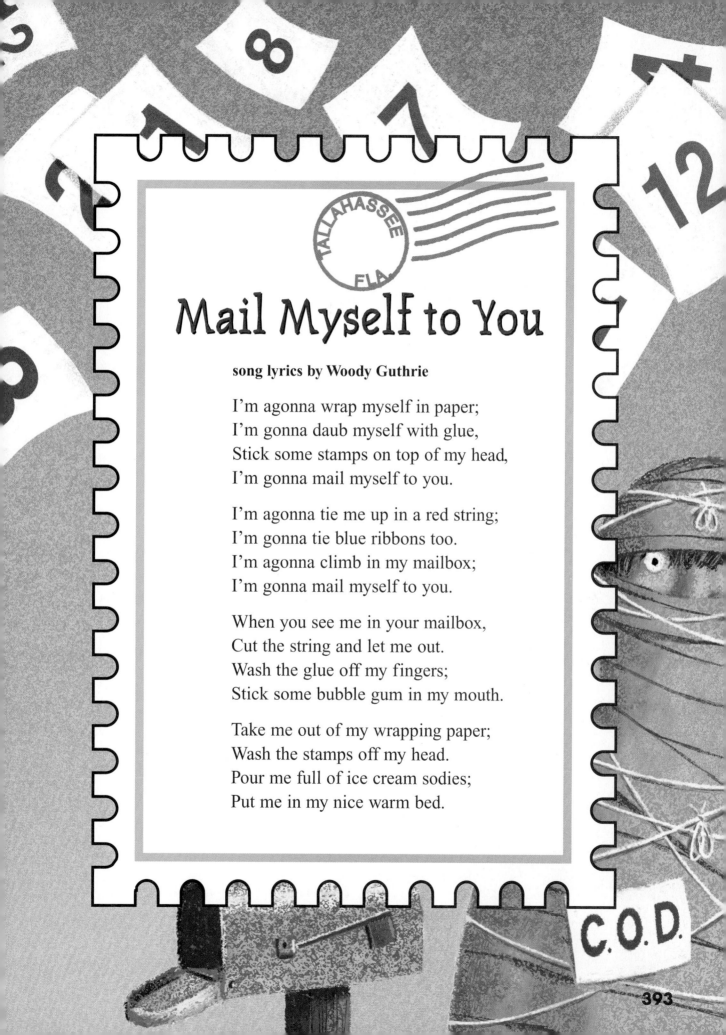

Mail Myself to You

song lyrics by Woody Guthrie

I'm agonna wrap myself in paper;
I'm gonna daub myself with glue,
Stick some stamps on top of my head,
I'm gonna mail myself to you.

I'm agonna tie me up in a red string;
I'm gonna tie blue ribbons too.
I'm agonna climb in my mailbox;
I'm gonna mail myself to you.

When you see me in your mailbox,
Cut the string and let me out.
Wash the glue off my fingers;
Stick some bubble gum in my mouth.

Take me out of my wrapping paper;
Wash the stamps off my head.
Pour me full of ice cream sodies;
Put me in my nice warm bed.

Wrap-Up

How many ways can we use our imaginations?

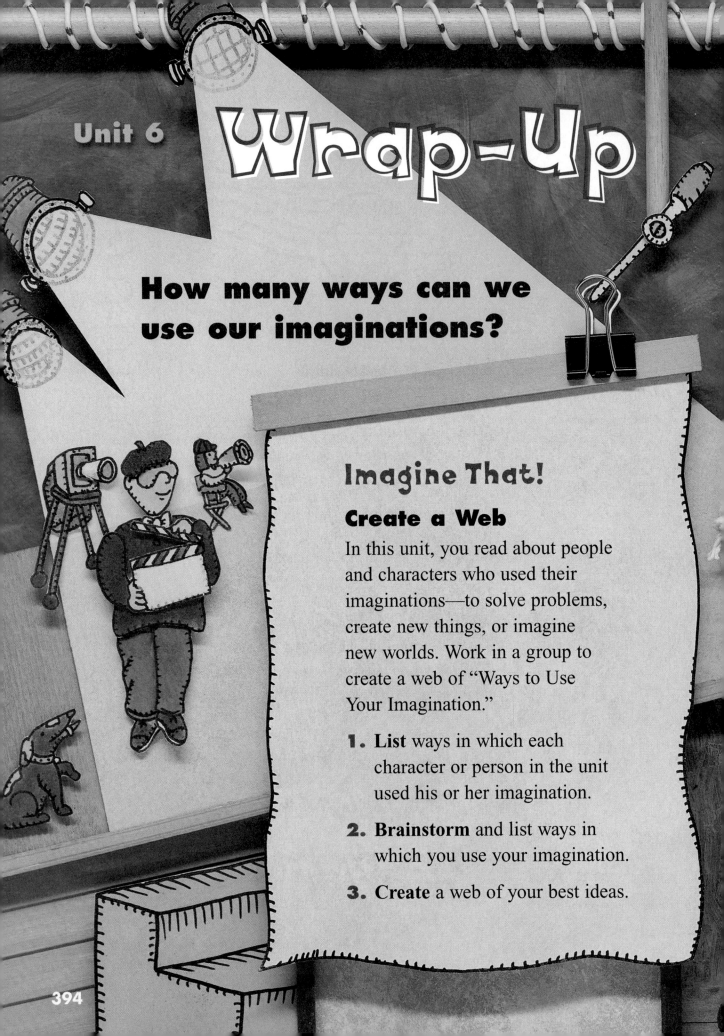

Imagine That!

Create a Web

In this unit, you read about people and characters who used their imaginations—to solve problems, create new things, or imagine new worlds. Work in a group to create a web of "Ways to Use Your Imagination."

1. **List** ways in which each character or person in the unit used his or her imagination.

2. **Brainstorm** and list ways in which you use your imagination.

3. **Create** a web of your best ideas.

Lights, Camera, Action!

Design a Set

Imagine that one of the selections in this unit is being made into a movie. You are the movie set designer!

1. **Choose** your favorite scene from one of the selections.

2. **Reread** the parts of the selection that describe the scene. As you read, list the details you want to include.

3. **Construct** a model of your movie set. Use boxes, posterboard, props, and paint to recreate the scene.

Where Am I?

Pantomime a Journey

Both Maxine in *Floating Home* and the two ants in *Two Bad Ants* travel to exciting new places. Pantomime a scene from one of the journeys.

1. Work with a partner. **Choose** a journey to pantomime.

2. **Reread** the selection and choose one scene. Practice acting out the events in the scene—without words!

3. **Perform** the pantomime for others. Can they guess your scene?

Problem Solved

Write a Letter

In *The Extra-Good Sunday,* Beezus and Ramona use their imaginations to prepare dinner. In *Mailing May,* Ma and Pa use their imaginations to send May to Grandma Mary's house. Imagine a different way to solve either Beezus and Ramona's or Ma and Pa's problem.

1. **Decide** whose problem you want to solve.

2. **Brainstorm** a new solution to the problem.

3. **Write** your solution in a friendly letter to the characters. Be sure to use proper letter form.

Test Talk

Answer the Question

Score High!

A scoring checklist shows you what makes up a good answer to a test question. You can learn how to write answers that score high by using a scoring checklist.

Read the scoring checklist at the right.

A test about "The Extra-Good Sunday," pages 323–337, might have this question.

Test Question 1

Compare how Ramona feels before she makes dinner to how she feels after she makes dinner. Use details from the story to support your answer.

Look at the First Try answer on page 397. Then see how the student used the scoring checklist to improve the answer.

Scoring Checklist

✓ **The answer is correct.** It has only correct details from the text.

✓ **The answer is complete.** It has all the necessary details from the text.

✓ **The answer is focused.** It has only details from the text that answer the question.

First Try

It's incorrect. The detail about skating is wrong.

> Before she makes dinner, Ramona combs her hair and cleans her room without being told. Then she goes out to skate. After she makes dinner, Ramona gives her mother a smile. Then she eats her pears.

It's not focused. This detail does not answer the question.

It's incomplete. It needs more details about Ramona's feelings.

Improved Answer

Tell why this is a better answer. Look back at the scoring checklist for help.

> Before she makes dinner, Ramona combs her hair and cleans her room without being told. She tries to be perfect to avoid cooking. After she makes dinner, Ramona gives her mother a shy smile. She feels lighter, and she is happy again.

Try it!

Now look at the First Try answer below. Then rewrite the answer and improve it. Look back at the scoring checklist for help.

Test Question 2

What did Beezus and Ramona do when they couldn't find a recipe for chicken thighs? Use details from pages 327–330 to support your answer.

First Try

When Beezus and Ramona couldn't find a recipe, they made up their own. They pulled off the skin and put the chicken in a dish. Then they put chili powder in yogurt and poured it over the chicken. They cooked the chicken in the oven.

Glossary

How to Use This Glossary

This glossary can help you understand and pronounce some of the words in this book. The entries in this glossary are in alphabetical order. There are guide words at the top of each page to show you the first and last words on the page. A pronunciation key is at the bottom of every other page. Remember, if you can't find the word you are looking for, ask for help or check a dictionary.

The entry word is in dark type. It shows how the word is spelled and how the word is divided into syllables.

The pronunciation is in parentheses. It also shows which syllables are stressed.

Part-of-speech labels show the function or functions of an entry word and any listed form of that word.

ar•rive (ə rīv′), VERB. to come to a place: *We arrived in Boston a week ago.* ❑ VERB **ar•rives, ar•rived, ar•riv•ing.**

Sometimes, irregular and other forms will be shown to help you use the word correctly.

The definition and example sentence show you what the word means and how it is used.

A a

al•pha•bet (al′fə bet), NOUN. the letters of a language arranged in a fixed order, not as they are in words. The English alphabet is: a b c d e f g h i j k l m n o p q r s t u v w x y z.

an•ten•na (an ten′ə), NOUN. one of the long, slender feelers on the heads of insects, crabs, lobsters, and shrimp: *That ant has only one antenna.* ❑ PLURAL **an•ten•nae** (an ten′ē) or **an•ten•nas.**

ap•pre•ci•ate (ə prē′shē āt), VERB. to be thankful for: *We appreciate your help in making the posters.* ❑ VERB **ap•pre•ci•ates, ap•pre•ci•at•ed, ap•pre•ci•at•ing.**

ar•rive (ə rīv′), VERB. to come to a place: *We arrived in Boston a week ago.* ❑ VERB **ar•rives, ar•rived, ar•riv•ing.**

as·ton·ish (ə ston′ish), VERB. to surprise greatly; amaze: *We were astonished at the force of the wind during the storm.* ❑ VERB **as·ton·ish·es, as·ton·ished, as·ton·ish·ing.**

as·tro·naut (as′trə nȯt), NOUN. a member of the crew of a spacecraft.

At·lan·tic (at lan′tik), NOUN. **Atlantic Ocean,** the ocean east of North and South America. It extends to Europe and Africa.

at·mo·sphere (at′mə sfir), NOUN. the air that surrounds Earth. Nitrogen and oxygen can be found in the atmosphere.

at·tempt (ə tempt′), VERB. to try: *I will attempt to draw a picture of myself.*

auc·tion (ȯk′shən), NOUN. a public sale in which each thing is sold to the person who offers the most money for it: *Grandma had an auction to sell many of her belongings.*

auc·tion·eer (ȯk′shə nir′), NOUN. someone whose business is conducting auctions: *The auctioneer was upset when the people made very low bids.*

av·e·nue (av′ə nü), NOUN. a street, usually wide or bordered with trees. ❑ PLURAL **av·e·nues.**

B b

bank (bangk), NOUN. a place of business for keeping, lending, exchanging, and sending out money: *She brought her money to the bank.* ❑ VERB **banks, banked, bank·ing.**

bar·rel (bar′əl), NOUN. a container with a round, flat top and bottom and sides that curve out slightly. Barrels are usually made of boards held together by hoops.

a	hat	ė	term	ô	order	ch	child		
ā	age	i	it	oi	oil	ng	long		a in about
ä	far	ī	ice	ou	out	sh	she		e in taken
â	care	o	hot	u	cup	th	thin	ə	i in pencil
e	let	ō	open	ù	put	ᵺ	then		o in lemon
ē	equal	ȯ	saw	ü	rule	zh	measure		u in circus

bar·ren (bar′ən), *ADJECTIVE.* not able to produce or support much life: *a barren desert; a barren field.*

ba·sin (bā′ sn), *NOUN.* all the land drained by a river and the streams that flow into the river: *The Mississippi basin runs from the Appalachian Mountains to the Rockies.*

bel·low (bel′ō), *VERB.* to make a loud, deep noise; roar: *He bellowed at the children who were trampling his flowers.*

blind·ing (blīn′ding), *ADJECTIVE.* terribly bright; making someone unable to see: *Suddenly a blinding light lit the darkened room.*

bolt (bōlt), *NOUN.* a flash of lightning: *We saw a bolt of lightning during the storm.*

bril·liant (bril′yənt), *ADJECTIVE.*

1 shining brightly; sparkling: *brilliant jewels, brilliant sunshine.*

2 having great ability or intelligence: *She is a brilliant mathematician.*

brood (brüd), *VERB.* to sit on eggs in order for them to hatch. Hens and other birds brood till the young are hatched.

bun·dle (bun′dl),

1 *NOUN.* a number of things tied or wrapped together.

2 *VERB.* to tie or wrap together; make into a bundle: *We bundled all our old newspapers for the school's paper drive.* ❏ *VERB* **bun·dles, bun·dled, bun·dling.**

C c

cab·in (kab′ən), *NOUN.* a small, roughly built house; hut: *We spent the summer in a small log cabin in the woods.*

ca·lam·i·ty (kə lam′ə tē), NOUN. a terrible thing that happens such as a flood, the loss of your sight or hearing, or the loss of your savings or property: *It was a calamity that the Youngs' house was destroyed by fire.* ❏ PLURAL **ca·lam·i·ties.**

cart (kärt), VERB. to carry in or as if in a cart: *They came and carted the trash away.* ❏ VERB **carts, cart·ed, cart·ing.**

cher·ish (cher′ish), VERB. to care for someone tenderly; treat with affection; aid or protect: *We cherished our dog.*

chore (chôr), NOUN. a small task or job that you have to do regularly: *Feeding our pets and washing the dishes are my daily chores.*

chug (chug), VERB. to make sounds like this while moving: *The train chugged along the tracks.* ❏ VERB **chugs, chugged, chug·ging.**

cock·pit (kok′pit′), NOUN. the place where the pilot sits in an airplane or spacecraft: *The pilot and her co-pilot went into the cockpit.*

col·lege (kol′ ij), NOUN. a school where you can study after high school that gives degrees or diplomas: *After I finish high school, I plan to go to college to become a teacher.*

col·o·ny (kol′ə nē), NOUN. a group of people who leave their own country and go to settle in another land, but who still remain citizens of their own country: *The United States of America began as thirteen colonies.* ❏ PLURAL **col·o·nies.**

com·mo·tion (kə mō′shən), NOUN. a noisy, violent disturbance: *Their fight caused quite a commotion in the hall.*

a	hat	ė	term	ô	order	ch	child		
ā	age	i	it	oi	oil	ng	long		a in about
ä	far	ī	ice	ou	out	sh	she		e in taken
â	care	o	hot	u	cup	th	thin	ə	i in pencil
e	let	ō	open	ù	put	ŦH	then		o in lemon
ē	equal	ò	saw	ü	rule	zh	measure		u in circus

com•pass (kum′pəs), NOUN. a device for showing directions, with a magnetic needle that always points to the north: *The hikers used compasses to guide their way.* ❏ PLURAL **com•pass•es.**

compass

com•pas•sion (kəm pash′ən), NOUN. pity; feeling sorry for someone's hardship and wanting to help; sympathy: *Compassion for the earthquake victims caused many people to make contributions.*

con•den•sa•tion (kon′den sā′shən), NOUN. the process of changing from a gas or a vapor to a liquid.

con•duc•tor (kən duk′tər), NOUN.
1 someone in charge of a train and its passengers. The conductor often collects tickets or fares.
2 something that transmits heat, electricity, light, or sound: *Copper wire is used as a conductor of electricity.*

cone (kōn), NOUN.
1 a solid object with a flat, round base that narrows to a point at the top.
2 a scaly growth that bears the seeds on many evergreen trees.

con•quer (kong′kər), VERB. to win in war; get by fighting: *The evil knights conquered the defenseless kingdom.* ❏ VERB **con•quers, con•quered, con•quer•ing.**

coop•er (kü′pər), NOUN. person who makes or repairs barrels: *Grandpa bought a barrel from those coopers.*

cre·ate (krē āt′), VERB. to make something which has not been made before: *I am creating a new recipe for Mom's birthday dinner.* ❑ VERB **cre·ates, cre·at·ed, cre·at·ing.**

cru·el (krü′əl), ADJECTIVE. ready to hurt others or to enjoy their suffering: *The cruel man kicked his dog.*

crys·tal (kris′tl), NOUN. a hard, solid piece of some substance that is naturally formed of flat surfaces and angles. Crystals can be small, like grains of salt, or large, like some kinds of stone.

crystals

cun·ning (kun′ing), ADJECTIVE. clever in deceiving; sly: *The cunning fox outwitted the dogs and got away.*

D d

de·cree (di krē′), VERB. to order or settle by authority: *The city government decreed that all dogs must be licensed.* ❑ VERB **de·crees, de·creed, de·cree·ing.**

de·light (di līt′), VERB. to please greatly: *The circus delighted us.* ❑ VERB **de·lights, de·light·ed, de·light·ing.**

de·sign (di zīn′), VERB. to make a first sketch of; plan out; arrange the form and color of: *My mother designed my coat and my grandmother made it.* ❑ VERB **de·signs, de·signed, de·sign·ing. –de·sign′er,** NOUN.

de·spair (di spâr′), NOUN. the complete loss of hope; a dreadful feeling that nothing good can happen to you: *Despair seized us as we felt the boat sinking.*

a hat	ė term	ô order	ch child	⎧a in about
ā age	i it	oi oil	ng long	⎪e in taken
ä far	ī ice	ou out	sh she	ə⎨i in pencil
â care	o hot	u cup	th thin	⎪o in lemon
e let	ō open	u̇ put	ŦH then	⎩u in circus
ē equal	ȯ saw	ü rule	zh measure	

des·ti·na·tion (des tə nā′shən), NOUN. the place to which a person or thing is going or is being sent: *Florida is a warm destination for a winter vacation.*

de·vour (di vour′), VERB. to eat something hungrily or greedily: *The lion devoured the zebra.*

dew·lap (dü′ lap), NOUN. the loose flap of skin under the throat of cattle and some other animals: *The cow's dewlap moved as it chewed its food.*

dig·ni·ty (dig′nə tē), NOUN. a proud and self-respecting manner or appearance: *The candidate kept her dignity during the noisy debate.*

dis·tance (dis′təns), NOUN. a place far away: *She saw a light in the distance.*

dis·taste (dis tāst′), NOUN. a feeling of dislike: *His distaste for carrots showed clearly on his face.*

do·ri (dȯ rē′), NOUN. (Japanese) street.

dou·ble (dub′əl), ADJECTIVE. twice as much, as large, or as strong: *They were given double pay for working on a holiday.*

drag·on (drag′ən), NOUN. (in stories) a huge, fierce animal supposed to look like a winged lizard with scales and claws, and often supposed to breathe out fire and smoke.

dragon

dress•mak•er (dres′mā′kər), NOUN. a person whose work is making women's or children's clothing: *A well-known dressmaker made the dress specially for her.*

drought (drout), NOUN. a long period of dry weather: *The fields were dry and dusty because of the drought.*

duch•ess (duch′is), NOUN. the wife or widow of a duke. ❏ PLURAL **duch•ess•es.**

duck•ling (duk′ling), NOUN. a young duck: *The ducklings followed their mother to the pond.*

dusk (dusk), NOUN. the time just before dark: *We eat dinner at dusk.*

dust (dust), NOUN. fine, dry, powdery earth: *Dust lay thick on the road.*

E e

ech•o (ek′ō), VERB. to be heard again: *The sound was echoing through the valley.* ❏ VERB **ech•oes, ech•oed, ech•o•ing.**

ed•i•ble (ed′ə bəl), ADJECTIVE. safe or good to eat: *Toadstools are not edible.*

e•mer•gen•cy (i mėr′jən sē), NOUN. a situation that calls for immediate action: *I keep tools in my car for use in an emergency.* ❏ PLURAL **e•mer•gen•cies.**

en•gine (en′jən), NOUN. a machine that changes energy from fuel, steam, water pressure, and so on, into motion and power. An engine is used to apply power to some work, such as running other machines.

a hat	ė term	ô order	ch child	⎧a in about
ā age	i it	oi oil	ng long	⎪e in taken
ä far	ī ice	ou out	sh she	ə⎨i in pencil
â care	o hot	u cup	th thin	⎪o in lemon
e let	ō open	ů put	ᴛʜ then	⎩u in circus
ē equal	ȯ saw	ü rule	zh measure	

e·vap·o·ra·tion (i vap′ə rā′shən), NOUN. the process of turning into a gas or vapor. Water returns to the atmosphere through evaporation.

ex·cite·ment (ek sīt′mənt), NOUN. an excited condition: *The birth of the new baby caused great excitement in the family.*

excitement

ex·plode (ek splōd′), VERB. to blow up; burst with a loud noise: *The firecrackers were exploding near us.* ❑ VERB **ex·plodes, ex·plod·ed, ex·plod·ing.**

ex·plor·er (ek splôr′ər), NOUN. someone who travels into unknown areas in order to discover new things: *Astronauts are explorers of outer space.*

Ff

fam·ine (fam′ən), NOUN. almost total lack of food in a region or among a group of people; a time of starvation: *The famine was prevented by shipments of food.*

fa·mous (fā′məs), ADJECTIVE. very well known; noted: *The famous singer was greeted by a large crowd.*

feast (fēst), NOUN. a big meal for some special occasion and for a number of guests; banquet: *We went to the wedding feast.*

fe·ver·ish (fē′vər ish), ADJECTIVE. having fever: *The feverish child was sent home from school.*

fi·es·ta (fē es′tə), NOUN. a festival, especially in a Spanish-speaking country or area. ❑ PLURAL **fi·es·tas.**

fire·crack·er (fīr′krak′ər), NOUN. a small tube of paper roll containing gunpowder and a fuse. Firecrackers explode with a loud noise.

flab·ber·gast·ed (flab′ər gas′tid), *VERB.* speechless with surprise; greatly astonished: *We were flabbergasted by the size of the fish.*

flight (flīt), *NOUN.* a trip in an aircraft: *We had an enjoyable flight.*

flush (flush), *VERB.* to blush; glow: *Her face flushed when they laughed at her.* ❑ *VERB* **flush·es, flushed, flush·ing.**

France (frans), *NOUN.* a large country in western Europe.

Gg

girth (gėrth), *NOUN.* a strap or band that keeps the saddle in place on a horse: *Wilson tightened the girth before he got on his horse.*

globe (glōb), *NOUN.* the Earth; world.

grain (grān), *NOUN.* the seed of wheat, oats, corn, rice, and other cereal grasses.

greed·y (grē′dē), *ADJECTIVE.* wanting more than your share of something: *The dictator was greedy for power and money.* ❑ *ADJECTIVE* **greed·i·er, greed·i·est.**

guest (gest), *NOUN.* a person who is received and entertained at someone else's home, club, and so on; visitor.

guest

a	hat	ė	term	ô	order	ch	child		a in about
ā	age	i	it	oi	oil	ng	long		e in taken
ä	far	ī	ice	ou	out	sh	she	ə	i in pencil
â	care	o	hot	u	cup	th	thin		o in lemon
e	let	ō	open	ů	put	ŦH	then		u in circus
ē	equal	ȯ	saw	ü	rule	zh	measure		

Hh

Hin·du (hin′ dü), *NOUN.* someone who believes in the Hindu religion: *The Hindus invented the numeral zero.* ❑ *PLURAL* **Hin·dus.**

ho·ri·zon (hə rī′zn), *NOUN.* the line where earth and sky seem to meet. You cannot see beyond the horizon.

howl (houl), *VERB.* to give a long, loud, sad cry: *Our dog often can be heard howling at night.* ❑ *VERB* **howls, howled, howl·ing.**

howl

hurl (hėrl), *VERB.* to throw something with great force: *She hurled a stone into the river.* ❑ *VERB* **hurls, hurled, hurl·ing.**

Ii

i·gua·na (i gwä′nə), *NOUN.* a large lizard with a row of spines along its back. The iguana is found in places that are hot and wet. ❑ *PLURAL* **i·gua·nas.**

in·sti·tute (in′stə tüt), *NOUN.* an organization for some special purpose. An art institute teaches or displays art. A technical school is often called an institute.

in·stru·ment (in′strə mənt), *NOUN.* a device for measuring, recording, or controlling something. Rulers and yardsticks are instruments for measuring distance.

in·ter·est (in′tər ist), *NOUN.* the money paid for the use of someone else's money: *They paid a lot of interest on the money they borrowed from the bank.*

Ll

la·bel (lā′bəl), NOUN. a piece of paper or cloth that is sewed, glued, or fastened to something. A label tells what something is, who it belongs to, or who made it.

lan·tern (lan′tərn), NOUN. a portable lamp with transparent covering around it to protect it from rain or wind: *We used a lantern to light our way.*

launch (lȯnch), VERB. to send something out into the air with force: *They will launch the satellite in a rocket.* ❏ VERB **launch·es, launched, launch·ing.**

launch

learn (lėrn), VERB. to gain knowledge or skill: *We are learning a lot at school.* ❏ VERB **learns, learned, learn·ing.**

ledge (lej), NOUN. a narrow shelf: *My cat loves to sit on the window ledge.*

lib·er·al arts (lib′ər əl ärts), ADJECTIVE. a range of courses at a college that provides general knowledge: *The students took liberal arts courses such as history, math, and English.*

light·ning (līt′ning), NOUN. a flash of electricity in the sky. The sound that it makes is thunder.

liz·ard (liz′ərd), NOUN. a reptile that has scaly skin, four legs, and a narrow body: *They watched the lizard climb along the branch.* **–liz·ard·like,** ADJECTIVE.

lo·co·mo·tive (lō kə mō′ tiv), NOUN. a large engine that moves from place to place under its own power, used to pull railroad trains: *The locomotive pulled ten railroad cars.*

a	hat	ė	term	ô	order	ch	child		a in about
ā	age	i	it	oi	oil	ng	long		e in taken
ä	far	ī	ice	ou	out	sh	she	ə	i in pencil
â	care	o	hot	u	cup	th	thin		o in lemon
e	let	ō	open	ů	put	₮H	then		u in circus
ē	equal	ȯ	saw	ü	rule	zh	measure		

luck•y (luk′ē), ADJECTIVE. having or bringing good luck: *I think I am a very lucky person. My team always wins when I wear my lucky hat.* ❑ ADJECTIVE **luck•i•er, luck•i•est.**

lus•cious (lush′əs), ADJECTIVE. very pleasing to taste, smell, hear, see, or feel: *a painting of luscious colors.*

Mm

mag•ic (maj′ik), NOUN.
1 the skill of seeming to make things appear, disappear, or change into something else; performing tricks that seem to be impossible: *The magician made rabbits appear out of the hat by magic.*
2 something that produces results as if by magic; mysterious influence; unexplained power: *The magic of music made us feel rested and happy.*

magic

mail (māl), VERB. to send by way of the post office; put in a mailbox: *I am mailing a letter to you.* ❑ VERB **mails, mailed, mail•ing.**

meas•ure (mezh′ər), VERB. to find the size or amount of something; find how long, wide, deep, large, or much something is: *We measured the amount of water in the pail and found that it was two liters.* ❑ VERB **meas•ures, meas•ured, meas•ur•ing.**

mis•sion (mish′ ən), NOUN. an errand or task that people are sent somewhere to do: *He was sent on a mission to find the pilot of the jet that crashed.*

mix•ture (miks′chər), NOUN. something that has been mixed: *The yellow and blue paint were combined to make a green mixture. Orange is a mixture of red and yellow.*

mon•soon (mon sün′), NOUN.

1 a powerful wind of the Indian Ocean and southern Asia. It blows from the southwest from April to October and from the northeast during the rest of the year.
2 a season during which this wind blows from the southwest, usually bringing heavy rains.

Nn

nav•i•gate (nav′ə gāt), VERB. to sail, manage, or steer a ship, aircraft, or rocket: *She can navigate the boat through the choppy waters.*
❑ VERB **nav•i•gates, nav•i•gat•ed, nav•i•gat•ing.**

nest (nest), NOUN. a kind of home that birds build out of twigs, leaves, mud, and the like. Birds lay their eggs and protect their young ones in nests.

nest

news•pa•per (nüz′pā′pər), NOUN. sheets of paper printed every day or week, telling the news and carrying advertisements, pictures, articles, and useful information.

nu•mer•al (nü′mər əl), NOUN. a figure or group of figures standing for a number. Examples of some numerals are 7, 25, and 463.

Oo

or•bit•er (ôr′bə tər), NOUN. something that orbits, especially an artificial satellite: *Scientists examined lunar data sent back by the orbiter.*

ox•y•gen (ok′sə jən), NOUN. an invisible gas that forms about one fifth of the air and one third of water. Oxygen is a chemical element. Animals and plants cannot live without oxygen.

a	hat	ė	term	ô	order	ch	child		a in about
ā	age	i	it	oi	oil	ng	long		e in taken
ä	far	ī	ice	ou	out	sh	she	ə	i in pencil
â	care	o	hot	u	cup	th	thin		o in lemon
e	let	ō	open	u̇	put	ᴛʜ	then		u in circus
ē	equal	ȯ	saw	ü	rule	zh	measure		

P p

pal·ace (pal′is), NOUN. a very large, grand house, especially the official home of a king or queen.

paste (pāst), NOUN. a mixture you use to stick things together. It is often made of flour and water boiled together.

pas·ture (pas′chər), NOUN. a grassy field where cattle, sheep, or horses can feed.

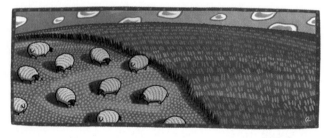

pasture

per·mis·si·ble (pər mis′ə bəl), ADJECTIVE. permitted; allowable: *It is permissible for my older sister to stay home alone.*

pig·eon·hole (pij′ ən hōl), NOUN. one of a set of boxlike spaces used to file or sort paper or letters: *The mailman put the letter in the correct pigeonhole.*

pi·ña·ta (pē nyä′tə), NOUN. a pot jar filled with candy, fruit, and small toys, hung at celebrations in Mexico and other Latin-American countries. Blindfolded children swing sticks in order to break the piñata to get what is inside.

place val·ue (plās val′ yü), NOUN. the value given to the place each digit in a number has. In 438, the place value of 4 is hundreds; the place value of 3 is tens; the place value of 8 is ones.

po·ny (pō′nē), NOUN. a kind of small horse. Ponies are usually less than 5 feet tall at the shoulder.
❑ PLURAL **po·nies.**

pool (pül), NOUN. a small pond: *There were frogs around the forest pool.*

post•al (pō′stəl), ADJECTIVE. of or about mail and post offices: *postal regulations, a postal clerk.*

pre•cip•i•ta•tion (pri sip′ə tā′shən), NOUN. the water that falls to the Earth in the form of rain, snow, sleet, or hail: *The forecast calls for some precipitation this afternoon.*

pres•sure (presh′ər), NOUN. the continued action of a weight or force: *The small box was flattened by the pressure of the heavy book.*

pro•ceed (prə sēd′), VERB. keep on doing something, especially after pausing for a short time: *After the time-out, we proceeded with the game.*

pro•nounce (prə nouns′), VERB. to say or make the sounds of a word; speak: *He pronounced that word differently than I did.* ❏ VERB **pro•nounc•es, pro•nounced, pro•nounc•ing.**

R r

ra•ja (rä′jə), NOUN. a ruler or chief in India and some other Eastern countries; rajah.

rec•i•pe (res′ə pē), NOUN. a set of written directions that show you how to fix something to eat: *Please give me your recipe for bread.* ❏ PLURAL **rec•i•pes.**

re•frig•e•ra•tor (ri frij′ə rā′tər), NOUN. an electrical appliance that keeps food or other things cold; fridge.

ref•uge (ref′yüj), NOUN. shelter or protection from danger or trouble.

re•solve (ri zolv′), VERB. to make up your mind about something: *I resolved to do better work in the future.* ❏ VERB **re•solves, re•solved, re•solv•ing.**

a	hat	ė	term	ô	order	ch	child		a in about
ā	age	i	it	oi	oil	ng	long		e in taken
ä	far	ī	ice	ou	out	sh	she	ə	i in pencil
â	care	o	hot	u	cup	th	thin		o in lemon
e	let	ō	open	ù	put	ŦH	then		u in circus
ē	equal	ò	saw	ü	rule	zh	measure		

rein (rān), NOUN. usually **reins,** long, narrow straps fastened to a bridle or bit, used to guide and control an animal: *When the rider pulled the rein to the right, the horse turned to the right.*

re•mark•a•ble (ri mär′kə bəl), ADJECTIVE. worth noticing because it is unusual: *He has a remarkable memory for names and faces.*

re•spect (ri spekt′), NOUN. a feeling of honor and admiration: *The children show great respect for their parents.*

respect

re•ward (ri wôrd′), NOUN. something you get in return for something that you have done: *A summer at camp was her reward for high grades.*

ridge (rij), NOUN. a long, narrow chain of hills or mountains: *We camped for a week on the Blue Ridge of the Appalachian Mountains.*

rid•ing sta•ble (rī′ding stā′bəl), NOUN. a place where horses are kept that provides instruction in horseback riding: *We learned to ride horses at the riding stable.*

route (rüt *or* rout), NOUN. a way that you choose to get somewhere: *Will you go to the coast by the northern route?*

rus•tle (rus′əl),
1 NOUN. a light, soft sound of things gently rubbing together: *The breeze caused rustling of the leaves.*
2 VERB. to make or cause to make this sound: *The leaves rustled in the wind.*
3 ADJECTIVE. making this sound: *I love the sound of rustling leaves.*
❑ VERB **rus•tles, rus•tled, rus•tling.**

S s

sad•dle (sad′l), NOUN. a seat for a rider on a horse's back, or on a bicycle or motorcycle.

saltworks (solt′wėrks′), NOUN. a plant where salt is made on a commercial scale.

sauce (sos), NOUN. something, usually a liquid, served with or on food to make it taste better.

scold (skōld), VERB. to speak to someone in an angry way: *She scolded the kids for making such a mess.* ❏ VERB **scolds, scold•ed, scold•ing.**

scout (skout), NOUN. someone who is sent out to get information: *The leader of the expedition sent a scout ahead of the group to look for water.*

self•ish (sel′fish), ADJECTIVE. caring too much for yourself and not enough for other people. Selfish people put their own interests first.

shone (shōn), VERB. a past tense of **shine:** *The sun shone all last week.*

sin•gle (sing′gəl), ADJECTIVE. only one: *The spider hung by a single thread.*

smear (smir), VERB. to cover or stain with anything sticky, greasy, or dirty: *My clothes are smeared with mud.*

snatch (snach), VERB. to seize something suddenly: *The hawk snatched the fish and flew away.* ❏ VERB **snatch•es, snatched, snatch•ing.**

soar (sôr), VERB. to fly at a great height; fly upward: *The eagle soars without flapping its wings.* ❏ VERB **soars, soared, soar•ing.** ■ Another word that sounds like this is **sore.**

soar

a	hat	ė	term	ô	order	ch	child		a in about
ā	age	i	it	oi	oil	ng	long		e in taken
ä	far	ī	ice	ou	out	sh	she	ə	i in pencil
â	care	o	hot	u	cup	th	thin		o in lemon
e	let	ō	open	ù	put	ŦH	then		u in circus
ē	equal	ȯ	saw	ü	rule	zh	measure		

sore (sôr), NOUN. a painful place on your body where the skin or flesh is broken or bruised. ■ Another word that sounds like this is **soar.**

space shut•tle (spās shut′l), NOUN. a spacecraft with wings, which can make a path around the Earth, land like an airplane, and be used again: *They watched as the space shuttle was sent into space.*

spar•kling (spär′kling), ADJECTIVE. shining; glittering: *Sparkling stars filled the night sky.*

sparkling

spied (spīd), VERB. the past participle of **spy:** *Who has spied on us?*

splash (splash), VERB. to cause water or another liquid to fly about and get people wet or dirty: *The swimmers like to splash each other with water.* ❑ VERB **splash•es, splashed, splash•ing.**

splash

spring (spring), NOUN. the season when plants begin to grow; season of the year between winter and summer.

star·tle (stär′tl), VERB. to frighten someone suddenly; surprise: *The dog jumped at the girl and startled her.*
❏ VERB **star·tles, star·tled, star·tling.**

startle

sta·tion (stā′shən), NOUN.
1 a regular stopping place along a route: *We'll get off at the next train station.*
2 a building or place used for a special reason: *The suspect was taken to the police station.*

stir·rup (stėr′ əp), NOUN. a loop or ring of metal or wood that hangs from a saddle to support a rider's foot: *She placed her foot in the stirrup before she began her ride.*

stock (stok), NOUN. the shares, or parts, owned in a company. The profits of a company, or the amount that is left after the bills are paid, are divided among the owners of stock.

stom·ach (stum′ək), NOUN. the large muscular bag in the body which receives food that is swallowed. The stomach digests some food before passing it on to the intestines.

store·house (stôr′hous′), NOUN. a place where things are stored: *After the harvest the storehouses were full.*
❏ PLURAL **store·hous·es.**

stum·ble (stum′bəl), VERB. to walk in an unsteady way: *As the tired hikers began to stumble, they knew it was time to rest.* ❏ VERB **stum·bles, stum·bled, stum·bling.**

stur·dy (stėr′dē), ADJECTIVE. strong: *She was a very sturdy child.*
❏ ADJECTIVE **stur·di·er, stur·di·est.**
–stur′di·ly, ADVERB.

a hat	ė term	ô order	ch child	a in about
ā age	i it	oi oil	ng long	e in taken
ä far	ī ice	ou out	sh she	ə ⟨ i in pencil
â care	o hot	u cup	th thin	o in lemon
e let	ō open	u̇ put	ᴛʜ then	u in circus
ē equal	ȯ saw	ü rule	zh measure	

suc•cess (sək ses′), *NOUN.* a result that you hoped and planned for: *Success in school comes from intelligence and hard work.* ❏ *PLURAL* **suc•cess•es.**

swan (swän), *NOUN.* a large, graceful water bird with a long, slender, curving neck. Adult swans are usually pure white.

swan

swift (swift), *ADJECTIVE.* moving very fast; able to move very fast: *The cowboy needed a swift horse.*

Tt

tail (tāl), *NOUN.* the part that sticks out from the back of an animal's body. Rabbits have short tails. Mice have long tails. ■ Another word that sounds like this is **tale.**

tale (tāl), *NOUN.* a story, either made-up or true: *We always enjoy hearing Grandfather's tales of his boyhood.* ■ Another word that sounds like this is **tail.**

thief (thēf), *NOUN.* someone who steals something: *A thief stole my bicycle from the yard.* ❏ *PLURAL* **thieves** (thēvs).

thirst (thėrst), *NOUN.* a dry, uncomfortable feeling in the mouth or throat caused by a need to have a drink: *She satisfied her thirst with a glass of water.*

thun•der (thun′dər), NOUN. the loud noise from the sky that comes after a flash of lightning. It is caused by a disturbance of the air resulting from the discharge of electricity.

trac•tor (trak′tər), NOUN. a heavy motor vehicle which moves on large rubber wheels. A tractor is used for pulling a wagon, plow, or other vehicle along roads or over fields.

traf•fic (traf′ik), NOUN. people, motor vehicles, ships, and so on coming and going along a way of travel: *Police control the traffic in large cities.*

treas•ure (trezh′ər), NOUN. valuable things, such as gold and jewels: *The pirates buried treasure along the coast.*

trench (trench), NOUN. a long, deep, narrow area like a valley or canyon in the ocean floor: *The deepest trench of the Pacific Ocean is much deeper than the Grand Canyon.* ❑ PLURAL **trench•es.**

trudge (truj), VERB. to walk wearily or with great effort: *She trudged slowly through the deep snow.* ❑ VERB **trudg•es, trudged, trudg•ing.**

twine (twīn), NOUN. a strong thread or string made of two or more strands twisted together: *We tied twine around the boxes to make sure they stayed shut.*

a	hat	ė	term	ô	order	ch	child	ə	a in about
ā	age	i	it	oi	oil	ng	long		e in taken
ä	far	ī	ice	ou	out	sh	she		i in pencil
â	care	o	hot	u	cup	th	thin		o in lemon
e	let	ō	open	ù	put	₮H	then		u in circus
ē	equal	ò	saw	ü	rule	zh	measure		

U u

un·nat·ur·al (un nach′ər əl), ADJECTIVE.
not normal; not natural: *It is
unnatural for a dog to climb a tree.*

un·u·su·al (un yü′zhü əl), ADJECTIVE.
not in common use; uncommon; rare:
Blue is an unusual color for food.
–un·u′su·al·ly, ADVERB.

unusual

W w

weath·er (weŦH′ər), NOUN. the
conditions of the air outside at a
certain place and time. Weather
includes facts about temperature,
wind, sun, rainfall, and so on.

weigh (wā), VERB. to have as a weight
of: *I weighed 110 pounds last year.*
❏ VERB **weighs, weighed,
weigh·ing.**

weight·less·ness (wāt′ lis nis), NOUN.
the quality of being free of the pull of
gravity: *Their weightlessness allowed
them to float in space.*

whip (wip), VERB. to move, put, or pull
something quickly and suddenly: *She
whipped off her coat.* ❏ VERB **whips,
whipped, whip·ping.**

whirl (wėrl), VERB. to turn or swing
round and round very fast; spin:
The leaves whirled in the wind.
❏ VERB **whirls, whirled, whirl·ing.**

whirl

wind[1] (wind), NOUN. air that is moving. The wind varies in force from a slight breeze to a strong gale.

wind[2] (wīnd), VERB. to move this way and that; change direction; turn: *A brook winds through the woods.* ❑ VERB **winds, wound, wind·ing.**

World War I (wėrld wôr wun), a war fought from 1914 to 1918. The United States, Great Britain, France, Russia, and their allies were on one side; Germany, Austria-Hungary, and their allies were on the other side.

worth·less (wėrth′lis), ADJECTIVE. useless: *Throw away those worthless, broken toys.*

a	hat	ė	term	ô	order	ch	child		
ā	age	i	it	oi	oil	ng	long		a in about
ä	far	ī	ice	ou	out	sh	she	ə	e in taken
â	care	o	hot	u	cup	th	thin		i in pencil
e	let	ō	open	ů	put	ŦH	then		o in lemon
ē	equal	ò	saw	ü	rule	zh	measure		u in circus

Handbook of Reading Skills

How to Use This Handbook

The following reading skills and definitions are found throughout your reading books. Understanding these skills can help you as you read. In this section, the skills are arranged in alphabetical order. Use these pages to help you review the terms and definitions. When reading, refer back to these pages as often as you need.

Author's Purpose

- The **author's purpose** is the author's reason for writing.

- An author's purpose may be to inform, to persuade, or to entertain.

- An author may also write to express a feeling about or set the mood of the scene.

Cause and Effect

- A **cause** is why something happens.

- An **effect** is what happens.

- Sometimes an author uses clue words, such as *so* and *because,* to tell what happens and why: *I went to bed early because I was tired.*

- When clue words are not present to signal cause and effect, look for what happens. Stop and think about why it happens.

Character

- A **character** is a person, thing, or animal in a story.

- Authors tell us about characters when they describe what characters say, do, and feel.

Compare and Contrast

- We **compare** when we say how things are alike.

- We **contrast** when we say how things are different.

- Clue words such as *yet* and *however* can signal a comparison or a contrast: *Cats and dogs are both mammals; however, they look very different.*

Context Clues

- **Context clues** can be used to figure out the meaning of a word.

- Often a context clue defines or explains the word. Look in the sentences or paragraph around an unknown word to help determine its meaning.

Drawing Conclusions

- A **conclusion** is a decision you make about what happens in a story.

- Authors give details about what happens. They may give clues about why things happen.

- You draw conclusions when you use what you know to make decisions that make sense about characters or events.

Fact and Opinion

- A **fact** can be proved true or false.

- An **opinion** is what someone believes or thinks and cannot be proved true or false.

- Words that express what someone thinks, such as *believe, could, like,* and *good,* are clues to a statement of opinion: *Chocolate ice cream is good.*

Generalizing

- A **generalization** is a statement or rule that applies to many examples.

- Sometimes you are given ideas about several things or people. A generalization might say how they are mostly alike or all alike in some way.

- Clue words, such as *all, always, everyone, some,* and *never,* can signal a generalization: *Everyone in my family has brown hair.*

Graphic Sources

- A **graphic source** can be a picture, diagram, map, chart, graph, or something else that shows information.

- Graphic sources show lots of information in an easy-to-see way.

- Making your own graphic can help you understand what you read.

Handbook of Reading Skills

Main Idea and Supporting Details

- The **main idea** is the most important idea of a paragraph or passage. It is sometimes stated.

- **Supporting details** are small pieces of information that tell more about the main idea.

Making Judgments

- A judgment is your opinion about a character, a situation, an action, or an idea in a story or article.

- When you **make judgments,** use what you already know and what you have read.

- Support your judgments with examples from the story or article.

Plot

- **Plot** includes the important events of a story that happen in the beginning, middle, and end, and how those events happen.

- Events that are important to the plot help keep the story going.

- A story map can help you keep track of the most important events in a story.

Predicting

- To **predict** means to tell what you think might happen next in a story, judging from what has already happened.

- A prediction is what you say might happen next.

- Use clues from the story and what you know from real life to help you make predictions.

- As you read, check and change your predictions based on new information.

Realism and Fantasy

- A **realistic** story tells about something that could happen in real life.

- A **fantasy** has some things that could happen and some things that could not happen.

Sequence

- **Sequence** is the order in which things happen in a story.

- Clue words, such as *before* and *after,* can tell you when something happens: *I will go to the store before I make the brownies.*

- Dates and times of the day can also tell you when something happens.

- Picture in your mind what is happening. If the order does not make sense, try to figure out an order that does.

Setting

- The **setting** is the time and place of a story.

- The setting can have an effect on how a character acts.

- An author may not always tell you where and when a story takes place. Look for clues in the art or words that point to the setting of a story.

Steps in a Process

- Following **steps in a process** usually means doing or making something in a certain order.

- Sometimes the steps are given in pictures as well as words.

- Sometimes there are clue words, such as *first, then,* or *the next step,* that help you with the order of these steps: *First, mix the batter. Then, pour it into a cake pan.*

Summarizing

- In a **summary,** a few sentences tell the main ideas of a story or article.

- To **summarize,** tell what the story is about without telling details.

Text Structure

- **Text structure** is the way a story or article is organized.

- One way an author can organize the text is to tell things in the order that they happen.

- Use what you know about story order to understand what you are reading.

Theme

- A **theme** of a story is the big idea of the story.

- When you read a story, think about what the writer wants you to learn from the story.

- You can use something from your own life to help you understand the theme or big idea.

Visualizing

- To **visualize** is to create pictures in your mind.

- You can put yourself into the story or article by using all of your senses.

- When you read, you may be able to use details in the text along with what you know about the subject to see, hear, smell, taste, and feel what the author describes.

Spelling Lists

Unit 4

Ananse's Feast

dream	dragon	drip	score
scared	scarf	coast	past
test	soft	left	gift
frown	frame	freeze	

Sam and the Lucky Money

squeeze	picture	caught	kept
different	surprise	favorite	chocolate
Tuesday	swimming	Monday	fifth
presents	easy	every	

Thunder Cake

enjoy	toys	royal	point
voice	noise	oil	true
due	glue	clue	who
movie	lose	move	

One Grain of Rice

that's	we're	it's	won't
I'm	he's	haven't	I'll
you'll	didn't	aren't	doesn't
let's	I've	they've	

The Woman Who Outshone the Sun

early	search	earth	heard
were	third	dirt	chirp
fur	nurse	turkey	Thursday
work	word	world	

Unit 5

Flight: The Journey of Charles Lindbergh

friends	crackers	miles	inches
marches	brushes	stitches	rushes
fixes	mixes	flies	tries
ladies	parties	pennies	

Chibi: A True Story from Japan

neck	trick	jacket	bucket
ticket	locker	brick	once
chance	face	since	police
house	erase	chase	

Brave Irene

unlucky	untie	unfold	unwrap
unhappy	unpack	unsafe	undo
repay	rewrite	refill	restart
replay	reread	repaint	

More Than Anything Else

started	smiled	cried	planned
hoped	fried	hopped	starting
smiling	crying	planning	hoping
frying	hopping		

Leah's Pony

where	what	when	wheel
whip	whale	while	want
was	watched	wear	went
warm	would	weep	

Unit 6

The Piñata Maker

wagon	lemon	open	garden
sugar	dollar	paper	another
brother	travel	squirrel	nickel
animal	final	real	

Mailing May

found	one	sure	until
always	almost	alone	a lot
doing	hasn't	couldn't	hadn't
angry	hungry	special	

Spelling Lists

The Extra-Good Sunday

walking	talk	chalk	stalk
drawing	straw	claws	awful
lawn	thaw	because	fault
sauce	haunted	cause	

Floating Home

fruit	friend	night	thought
does	again	said	people
believe	tried	tired	died
eight	Friday	Saturday	

Two Bad Ants

market	basket	wonder	monkey
mirror	order	before	tiger
relax	woman	bottle	apple
eagle	needle	candle	

Acknowledgments

Text

Page 12: From *Doctor Coyote* retold by John Bierhorst. Reprinted with the permission of Simon & Schuster Books for Young Readers, an imprint of Simon & Schuster Children's Publishing Division from *Doctor Coyote* retold by John Bierhorst. Text copyright © 1987 John Bierhorst.

Page 14: From *Ananse's Feast* by Tololwa M. Mollel. Text copyright © 1997 by Tololwa M. Mollel. Illustrations copyright © 1997 by Andrew Glass. Reprinted by permission of Clarion Books/Houghton Mifflin Company. All rights reserved.

Page 34: "The Fox and the Stork" from *Fifty Fabulous Fables* by Suzanne Barchers. © 1997 Libraries Unlimited. (800) 237-6124 or www.lu.com.

Page 38: Excerpt from *The Lost Lake* by Allen Say. Copyright © 1989 by Allen Say. Reprinted by permission of Houghton Mifflin Company. All rights reserved.

Page 40: *Sam and the Lucky Money* by Karen Chinn. Illustrated by Cornelius Van Wright & Ying-Hwa Hu. Text copyright © 1995 by Karen Chinn. Illustrations copyright © 1995 by Cornelius Van Wright and Ying-Hwa Hu. Reprinted by permission of Lee & Low Books, Inc.

Page 60: "What to Do with Money" from *A New True Book: Money* by Benjamin Elkin. Copyright © 1983 by Regensteiner Publishing Enterprises, Inc. Reprinted by permission.

Page 60: Figure "If you save just 50 cents a school day." Copyright © 1999 by Consumers Union of U.S., Inc. Yonkers, NY 10703–1057, a nonprofit organization. Reprinted with permission from the September/October 1999 issue of *Zillions*, for educational purposes only. No commercial use or photocopying permitted. Log onto www.zillions.org

Page 62: From *Fire!* by Caroline Evans. Copyright © 1995 by the National Wildlife Federation. Reprinted from the October 1995 issue of *Ranger Rick Magazine* with the permission of the publisher, the National Wildlife Federation.

Page 64: *Thunder Cake* by Patricia Polacco. Copyright © 1990 by Babushka, Inc. Reprinted by permission of Philomel Books, a division of Penguin Putnam, Inc.

Page 86: Excerpt and illustrations from *Firetalking* by Patricia Polacco. Text copyright © 1994 by Patricia Polacco. Reprinted by permission.

Page 88: Excerpt from *Darkness and the Butterfly* by Ann Grifalconi, 1987, pp. 1–6. Copyright © 1987 by Ann Grifalconi. Reprinted by permission of Little, Brown and Company.

Page 90: *One Grain of Rice: A Mathematical Folktale* by Demi. Published by Scholastic Press, a division of Scholastic, Inc. Copyright © 1997 by Demi. Reprinted by permission of Scholastic, Inc.

Page 113: "Numerals Today" from *A New True Book: Numbers* by Philip Carona. Copyright © 1982 by Regensteiner Publishing Enterprises, Inc. Reprinted by permission.

Page 116: From *Uncle Nacho's Hat* by Harriet Rohmer. Reprinted with permission of the publisher, Children's Book Press, San Francisco, CA. Copyright © 1998 by Harriet Rohmer.

Page 118: *The Woman Who Outshone the Sun* by Alejandro Cruz Martinez. Reprinted with permission of the publisher, Children's Book Press, San Francisco, CA. Story copyright © 1991 by Children's Book Press and Rosalma Zubizarreta. Pictures copyright © 1991 by Fernando Olivera.

Page 136: "Iguana" from *Amazing Lizards* by Trevor Smith. Copyright © 1990 by Alfred A. Knopf. Reprinted by permission.

Page 138: *Going Through the Old Photos* by Michael Rosen. Reprinted by permission of PFD on behalf of Michael Rosen. © 1979 Michael Rosen

Page 139: "Quilt" from *A Suitcase of Seaweed* by Janet S. Wong. Reprinted with permission of Margaret K. McElderry Books, an imprint of Simon & Schuster Children's Publishing Division from *A Suitcase of Seaweed* by Janet S. Wong. Copyright © 1996 Janet S. Wong.

Page 140: "The Stars/Las estrellas" from *Grandmother's Nursery Rhymes,* Text © 1994 by Nelly Palacio Jaramillo. Translation © 1994 by Raquel Jaramillo. Reprinted by permission of Henry Holt and Company, Inc.

Page 141: "Sky Bear" from *The Earth Under Sky Bear's Feet* by Joseph Bruchac, 1995. Copyright © by Joseph Bruchac. Reprinted by permission of Penguin Putnam, Inc.

Page 148: From *Grandpa Is a Flyer* by Sanna Anderson Baker. Text copyright © 1995 by Sanna Anderson Baker. Excerpt reprinted by permission of Albert Whitman & Company.

Page 150: *Flight: The Journey of Charles Lindbergh* by Robert Burleigh. Text copyright © 1991 by Robert Burleigh. Illustrations copyright © 1991 by Mike Wimmer. Used by permission of Philomel Books, a division of Penguin Putnam, Inc.

Page 172: From "Moving Along on Bike Trails" by Stewart Warren, *The Herald News,* August 5, 1998. Reprinted by permission of *The Herald News,* Joliet, IL.

Page 174: Chapter One from *Chibi: A True Story from Japan* by Barbara Brenner and Julia Takaya. Text copyright © 1996 by Barbara Brenner and Julia Takaya. Illustrations copyright © 1996 by June Otani. Reprinted by permission of Clarion Books/Houghton Mifflin Company. All rights reserved.

Page 196: "The Physical World" from *Student Atlas.* Copyright © 1998 by DK Publishing, Inc. Reprinted by permission.

Page 198: From *A Little Excitement* by Marc Harshman. Text copyright © 1989 by Marc Harshman. Reprinted by permission of Cobblehill Books, an affiliate of Dutton Children's Books, a division of Penguin Putnam, Inc.

Page 200: *Brave Irene* by William Steig. Copyright © 1986 by William Steig. Reprinted by permission of Farrar, Straus & Giroux, LLC.

Page 221: "Water on Earth" by David Heil, et al. From *Discover the Wonder.* Copyright © 1996 Scott, Foresman and Company, Glenview, Illinois.

Page 224: From *Tomás and the Library Lady* by Pat Mora, copyright © 1997 by Pat Mora. Used by permission of Alfred A. Knopf Children's Books, a division of Random House, Inc.

Page 227: From *More Than Anything Else* by Marie Bradby, illustrated by Chris K. Soentpiet. Published by Orchard Books, an imprint of Scholastic Inc. Text copyright © 1995 by Marie Bradby, illustrations copyright © 1995 by Chris K. Soentpiet. Reprinted by permission of Scholastic Inc.

Page 244: Excerpts from "$1.50 and a Dream" by Toni A. Watson, *Cobblestone,* February, 1996. Copyright © 1996 by Cobblestone Publishing, Inc. Reprinted by permission.

Page 246: Excerpt from *Popsicle Pony* by Jill Stover, 1994, pp. 1–8. Copyright © 1994 by Jill Stover. Used by permission of HarperCollins Publishers.

Page 248: *Leah's Pony* by Elizabeth Friedrich. Illustrated by Michael Garland. Text copyright © 1996 by Elizabeth Friedrich. Illustrations copyright © by Michael Garland. All rights reserved. Reprinted by permission of Boyds Mills Press, Inc.

Page 266: Excerpts from "Giddyap!" by Sarah Bourdelais, *U.S. Kids,* June, 1999. Copyright © 1999 by Children's Better Health Institute, Benjamin Franklin Literary & Medical Society, Inc. Reprinted by permission.

Page 267: Illustration for the entry Horse from *The World Book Encyclopedia,* 1997. Reprinted by permission.

Page 268: "At the Library" from *It's Raining Laughter* by Nikki Grimes. Copyright © 1997 by Nikki Grimes. Reprinted by permission of Dial Books for Young Readers, a division of Penguin Putnam, Inc.

Page 268: "A Book" from *My Head Is Red and Other Riddle Rhymes* by Myra Cohn Livingston. Copyright © 1990 by Myra Cohn Livingston. Reprinted by permission of Marian Reiner.

Page 269: "Somewhere" from *Is Somewhere Always Far Away?* by Leland B. Jacobs. Copyright © 1993 by Allan D. Jacobs. Reprinted by permission of Henry Holt and Company, Inc.

Page 270: "Let's send a rocket" from *Poems to Me* by Kit Patrickson. © 1978 by Ginn and Company, reprinted by permission of Silver Burdett Ginn.

Page 271: "The Moon, a Banana" by Jesús Carlos Soto Morfín. English version translated by Judith Infante. Translation © copyright Judith Infante. Reprinted by permission of Judith Infante.

Page 278: From *Tate Gallery Drawing: A Young Artist's Guide* by Jude Welton. Copyright © 1994 Dorling Kindersley Limited, London. Text copyright © 1994 Jude Welton. Reprinted by permission of Dorling Kindersley, New York.

Page 280: Excerpts adapted from *The Piñata Maker/El Piñatero* by George Ancona. Copyright © 1994 by George Ancona. Reprinted by permission of Harcourt Brace & Company.

Page 295: "Southwest Settlements" from *Social Studies Communities Around Us* by J.R. Garcia, D.J. Gelo, L.L. Greenow, K.B. Kracht, D.G. White. © 1997 by Silver Burdett Ginn, Simon & Schuster Education Group. Used by permission.

Page: 298: Excerpt from *Bonanza Girl* by Patricia Beatty. Copyright © 1987 by Patricia Beatty. Used by permission of HarperCollins Publishers.

Page 300: *Mailing May* by Michael O. Tunnell, illustrated by Ted Rand. Text copyright © 1997 by Michael O. Tunnell. Used by permission of Greenwillow Books.

Page 318: "Post Haste" from *Train* by John Coiley. Copyright © 2000 by Dorling Kindersley. Reprinted by permission.

Page 320: From *You Can't Eat Your Chicken Pox, Amber Brown* by Paula Danziger. Copyright © 1995 by Paula Danziger. Reprinted by permission of G. P. Putnam's Sons, a division of Penguin Putnam, Inc.

Page 322: "The Extra-Good Sunday" from *Ramona Quimby, Age 8* by Beverly Cleary. Copyright © 1981 by Beverly Cleary. Used by permission of HarperCollins Publishers.

Page 340: "A Pizza the Size of the Sun" by Jack Prelutsky from *Food Fight,* edited and illustrated by Michael J. Rosen. Copyright © 1994 by Jack Prelutsky. Reprinted by permission.

Page 342: Excerpt from *Grandpa Takes Me to the Moon* by Timothy R. Gaffney, pp. 1–7. Copyright © 1996 by Timothy R. Gaffney. Used by permission of HarperCollins Publishers.

Page 344: From *Floating Home* by David Getz. Text copyright © 1997 by David Getz. Illustrations copyright © 1997 by Michael Rex. Reprinted by permission of Henry Holt and Company, Inc.

Page 364: Excerpts from "Spacewalk Talk: Interview with Astronaut Chris Hadfield" from *Owl,* May, 2000. Copyright © 2000 by Bayard Press. Reprinted by permission.

Page 366: From *The Girl Who Wore Snakes* by Angela Johnson. Published by Orchard Books, an imprint of Scholastic Inc. Copyright © 1993 by Angela Johnson.

Reprinted by permission of Scholastic Inc.

Page 367: From *Verdi* by Janell Cannon. Copyright © 1997 by Janell Cannon. Reprinted by permission of Harcourt Brace & Company.

Page 368: *Two Bad Ants.* Copyright © 1988 by Chris Van Allsburg. Reprinted by permission of Houghton Mifflin Company. All rights reserved.

Page 386: "Pandora's Box" from *The Robber Baby* by Anne Rockwell. Copyright © 1994 by Anne Rockwell. Used by permission of HarperCollins Publishers.

Page 390: "The Limerick's Lively to Write" from *One at a Time* by David McCord. Copyright 1925, 1929, 1931, 1941, 1949, 1952, © 1961, 1962, 1965, 1966, 1968, 1970, 1971, 1972, 1973, 1974 by David McCord. Reprinted by permission of Little, Brown and Company.

Page 391: "I Love the Look of Words" by Maya Angelou. Text copyright © 1993 by Maya Angelou. Illustration for "I Love the Look of Words" by Tom Feelings. Illustration copyright © 1993 by Tom Feelings. From *Soul Looks Back in Wonder* by Tom Feelings. Reprinted by permission of Dial Books for Young Readers, a division of Penguin Putnam, Inc.

Page 392: "Hugs and Kisses" from *The Tamarindo Puppy* by Charlotte Pomerantz. Text Copyright © 1980 by Charlotte Pomerantz. Reprinted by permission of HarperCollins Publishers.

Page 393: "Mail Myself to You" words and music by Woody Guthrie. TRO-© copyright 1962 (renewed) and 1963 (renewed) Ludlow Music, Inc., New York, New York. Reprinted by permission of the Richmond Organization.

Selected text and images in this book are copyrighted © 2002.

Artists

Cover: Jui Ishida

Pages 12–13: Lee Lee Brazeal

Pages 14–33: Andrew Glass

Pages 34–37: Karen Blessen

Pages 40–59: Cornelius Van Wright and Ying-Hwa Hu

Pages 60–61, 144–145, 274–275, 396–397: Tony Klassen

Pages 62–83, 87: Patricia Polacco

Pages 64, 84: Margaret Cusak

Pages 88–89: Lisa Adams

Pages 90–112: Demi

Pages 113–115: Kris Wiltse

Pages 116–117, 394–395: Franklin Hammond

Pages 4, 6, 118–135, 426: Fernando Olivera

Pages 140–141: Pat Maire

Pages 142–143: Margaret Kasahara

Pages 146–147: Maryjane Begin

Pages 148–149: Burgandy Beam

Pages 150–167: Mike Wimmer

Pages 169–171, 198–199: Todd Leonardo

Pages 172–173: Roberta Ludlow

Pages 6, 174–195, 427, 428: June Otani

Pages 200–220: William Steig

Pages 224–225: Jeremy Tugeau

Pages 226–242: Chris K. Soentpiet

Pages 246–247: Laura Ovresat

Pages 248–265: Michael Garland

Pages 266–267: Tom Newsom

Pages 268–271: Chris Gall

Pages 272–273: Alison Jay

Pages 276–277: Blair Drawson

Pages 8, 300–315, 429, 430: Ted Rand

Pages 316–317: Sharon Hoogstraten

Pages 322–339: Susan Spellman

Pages 340–341: Dave Jonason

Pages 342–343: Dee Deloy

Pages 344–363: Michael Rex

Pages 368–383: Chris Van Allsburg

Pages 386–389: Anne Rockwell

Pages 390–393: Mike Reed

Photographs

Every effort has been made to secure permission and provide appropriate credit for photographic material. The publisher deeply regrets any omission and pledges to correct, in subsequent editions, errors called to its attention.

Unless otherwise acknowledged, all photographs are the property of Scott Foresman, a division of Pearson Education. Page abbreviations are as follows: (t) top, (b) bottom, (l) left, (r) right, (ins) inset, (s) spot, (bk) background.

Page 10–11: Doug Armand/Stone

Page 32: Courtesy Tololwa M. Mollel

Pages 38–39, 278–279, 298–299, 336–337: Sharon Hoogstraten

Page 58: (ALL) Courtesy, Lee & Low Books

Pages 62–63: Jeff Henry

Page 63: (INSET) Stan Osolinski/Dembinsky Photo Assoc. Inc.

Pages 84, 86 (T), 87 (BL): © Lawrence Migdale/www.migdale.com

Page 86: (TC) Patricia Polacco

Page 111: Courtesy, Henry Holt and Company, Inc.

Page 134: Courtesy, Children's Book Press

Pages 136, 137: (ALL) © Dorling Kindersley

Pages 159, 221–222, 368: (T) PhotoDisc

Page 167: (ALL) Molly Levite Griffis Courtesy of Levite of Apache

Page 168: © Bettmann/Corbis

Page 169, 171 (T): Lilly Library

Page 170: Photo Collection/Los Angeles Public Library

Page 194: (B) Courtesy of Julia Takaya; (T) Courtesy Barbara Brenner

Pages 196, 197 (BR): © Dorling Kindersley

Page 219: Photo: Anne Hall/ Courtesy Farrar, Straus & Giroux, Inc.

Page 242: (B) Courtesy Chris Soentpiet; (T) Courtesy, Orchard Books

Page 244: © Charles A. Harris/Corbis

Page 245: FLORIDA STATE ARCHIVES

Page 264: Richard Hutchings for Scott Foresman

Pages 276–277: From *Mary Margaret's Tree* by Blair Drawson. Copyright © 1996 by Blair Drawson. U. S. copyright: Reprinted by permission of the publisher, Orchard Books, New York. Canadian copyright: Published in Canada by Groundwood Books

Pages 281–294: George Ancona

Pages 295: Laurence Parent

Page 296: The Granger Collection, New York

Page 297: David Carriere/Stone

Page 316: (ALL) Courtesy, William Morrow

Page 318: (B) London Transport Museum/ © Dorling Kindersley

Page 319: (TL) Culver Pictures Inc.; (TR) Millbrook House Ltd.; (BR) ET Archive

Pages 320–321: Janet Gill/Stone

Page 338: Courtesy, William Morrow

Page 362: (T) Courtesy David Getz; (B) Courtesy Michael C. Rex

Page 364: (Both) Chip Simon

Page 365: (T) © NASA/Roger Ressmeyer/Corbis

Page 384: AP/Wide World

Page 400: (B) Mark A. Schneider/Visuals Unlimited

Page 403: SuperStock

Page 404: NASA

Page 406: Gregory Gorel/Visuals Unlimited

Page 408: Gary Conner/PhotoEdit

Page 410: Joe McDonald/Visuals Unlimited

Page 413: Pool/Liason Agency

Glossary

The contents of the glossary have been adapted from *Thorndike Barnhart Dictionary, Beginning Level,* copyright © 1999, Addison Wesley Educational Publishers, Inc., Glenview, Illinois and *Thorndike Barnhart Children's Dictionary* © 2001, 1999 Scott Foresman, a division of Addison-Wesley Educational Publishers, Inc.